YES I CAN

YES I CAN

AN ARMY NURSE'S STORY BEFORE, DURING AND AFTER DESERT STORM IN SAUDI ARABIA

LORETTA SCOTT

Copyright © 2005 by Loretta Scott.

Library of Congress Number: 2005900299
ISBN :   Hardcover   1-4134-6532-3
           Softcover   1-4134-6531-5

Editing by IHOW Publishing,
Lithonia, Georgia

Graphic Design by FATCATDESIGN,
Marrietta, Georgia

All rights reserved. No part of this book may be reproduced or transmitted in any form or by any means, electronic or mechanical, including photocopying, recording, or by any information storage and retrieval system, without permission in writing from the copyright owner.

This book contains the story of the author, these are her opinions and experiences. Names in this book have been changed to protect the privacy of the individuals.

This book was printed in the United States of America.

To order additional copies of this book, contact:
Xlibris Corporation
1-888-795-4274
www.Xlibris.com
Orders@Xlibris.com

Contents

Acknowledgments 9
Preface 13
Chapter 1: Leaving Home 17
Chapter 2: Beginning Training 23
Chapter 3: Training At The Mobilization Site 29
Chapter 4: Training, Training, Training 32
Chapter 5: The Plunge Or The Beginning 42
Chapter 6: The Landing, War Or Defeat 48
Chapter 7: In Saudi 51
Chapter 8: The Desolate 57
Chapter 9: The Desert & The Storm 69
Chapter 10: We're Ready 79
Chapter 11: Making A Connection 86
Chapter 12: Getting Closer 88
Chapter 13: Depmeds 93
Chapter 14: Ground War 99
Chapter 15: War Gossip Or Simply Just Rumours? 116
Chapter 16: Departing Friendship 120
Chapter 17: Mail Call, The Forgotten Soldier 123
Chapter 18: "Cease Fire", The War Is Over 124
Chapter 19: "At Ease" 127
Chapter 20: "Palm Sunday" 137

Chapter 21: The Wait 141
Chapter 22: "Easter" 150
Chapter 23: "Are You Ready?" 153
Chapter 24: The Calling, Going Home 156
Chapter 25: Home 165
Chapter 26: "The Disaster" 184
Chapter 27: Departing Intimacy 190
Chapter 28: "It's Over" 202
Chapter 29: Falling Apart 206
Chapter 30: "Relocation, I Can Do This" 227
Chapter 31: "Finding Peace" 232
Chapter 32: "Returning To Florida" 240
Chapter 33: "Reality Shock" 249
Chapter 34: Finding My Soulmate 253
Chapter 35: "At Last" 258
Epilougue 259
Abbreviation List 261

Dedication

To my Mother, her strength taught me to survive anything and to believe in myself. To my Father, whose Army experience taught me to keep my guard up, and to never volunteer, and I would make it. To my deceased sister, who said, "To gain is to conquer, but to lose is to gain, there is no such thing called luck." To my deceased brother, who would have said, "Life is full of many obstacles, but only you can set yourself free." To my grandmother for positive talks when no one else listened, and the encouragement of I can conquer anything. Also, to Cpt. Gretchen Stretchen aka Weenie for her constant friendship and support.

Acknowledgments

To my precious **LORD JESUS CHRIST** for his unwavering grace through the storm.

To my daughter LAKISHA, I thank you for being the sweet kind person that you are, for your obedience and for helping the family when I needed you most-during the crisis.

To my sons, JOSEPH and GARLAND, I thank you both for your love and understanding and for supporting the family during the storm.

To LAKIVEA, thank you for the second pair of eyes and your support and encouragement to make the book a success.

To GEORGE, thank you for your support, guidance and love, I love you.

To IIIOW PUBLISHING, Marsha for your steadfast constructive criticisms, strength, and your ability to edited the book, thank you.

To ZAHIRA, I thank you for giving me the insight that yes I can write. I thank you for your encouragement and the ideas to go ahead and do it. Well done.

To JERIS, for your love and support during the times when no one else seemed to care. I thank you for your intellectual input, compassion, your shoulder when I cried, and undying words that gave me the go-ahead to write, and the Yes, I did it!

To JESSIE, for your unwavering love, support, strength and encouragement when I wanted to say, "I can't do it." I thank you for your love and patience, and most of all for believing in me, and never doubting that I couldn't write.

To all the SOLDIERS, who fought a good race and endured the pain and frustrations as I did. We claim victory for a job well-done.

To the FAMILIES who lost their love ones and supported the troops. I thank you all for your unconditional love and your loved ones' bravery. My gratitude to you all.

"We must always keep in mind that the army must be prepared to fight, that fighting is tough, and that it takes strong discipline and highly motivated men to fight and live. This is the balance we must strike-Discipline and Motivation; we must build on both. This is the heart of the army on this we cannot compromise."

Williams C. Westmoreland
General, USA, 1970

Special Dedication Page

The only P.O.W. missing from the **Gulf War**

Name: Michael Scott Speicher
Rank at Loss/Branch: Lt.Cdr./US Navy
Rank in 2002: Commander
Unit: USS SARATOGA
Age at Loss: 33,
Born: March 1958
Age in 2003: 47
Home City of Record: Jacksonville FL
Date of Loss: 17 January 1991
Country of Loss: Unknown

**OPERATION IRAQI FREEDOM
CAPTURED AND RESCUED POW'S**

SHOSHANA JOHNSON
Spec / US Army

JESSICA LYNCH
Pfc / US Army

VIETNAM WAR

LYNDA VAN DEVANTER
US Army Nurse in Vietnam whose autobiography focused attention on women's struggles with post traumatic stress syndrome and chemicals including Agent Orange.

Gulf War

CPT Robert L Thibodeau, RN for pictures

Cpt Gretchen Stretchen (Weenie) for her special friendship

Preface

The true definition of the word "War" per various defining sources is: "A state of open, armed, often prolonged conflict carried on between nations, states, or parties." And a true definition of the word "Nurse" per various defining sources is: "A person educated and trained to care for the sick or disabled." I chose to become a part of the second definition. My main being in life besides that of a family member is to help another human being to become well or to assist them to gain the ability to care for themselves doing their disabling times. Never would I have thought that my career would have taken me into the vials of pure hell! But, it did. Not after I became an adult in a world that sometimes seems unfair. Not after I became a member of my country's armed forces. But after I went to live up to my responsibilities as an Army Nurse to assist those in need; did such a saddening of events occur. Events that I sometimes would prefer to forget. Events that won't stay out of my memory. Events that were at times enjoyable and others not worth the seconds or minutes they took to become processed.

This is my story; this is the person I am. This is the person I became. This is the person I shall remain to be . . . "An Army Nurse" proud to have provided the best service I could have in disastrous times when your daily routine 24/7 was often to work while wearing gas masks. Or in strenuous times when the casualties from all sides would mount and you would find yourself working on persons from other countries, such as the enemies' whose hygienic way of cleaning themselves was by using their hands instead of tissue. Or in less patient times when the anxiety of participation to get this war finally started and over with would put you in the role of confidant to your peers and them to you.

This story welcomes you to find the inner strength to say regardless what comes along in life I can beat this obstacle . . . "Yes I Can!"

I Am A Soldier

It doesn't matter who I am. I am a soldier and I am called to fight for my country.
It doesn't matter who I am. I am a soldier and I am called to leave my children.
I am called to fight for my country.
It doesn't matter who I am. I am a soldier who has been trained to defend my country.
It doesn't matter who I am. I must get my business in order in a short notice; I am called to fight for my country.
It doesn't matter who I am. I'm a soldier.
I must travel to a strange land for no given reason; I am called to fight for my country.
It doesn't matter who I am. I am a soldier. I must adjust to foreign customs. I am called to fight for my country.
It doesn't matter who I am. I'm a soldier.
I must adjust to my environment; I must survive.
I am called to fight for my country.
It doesn't matter who I am.
I'm a soldier.
I must return to the civilian world to be called a hero or heroine.
I have defended my country and victory has been bestowed.

"I AM A SOLDIER."

Written by: Loretta Swinney-Scott

Chapter 1

Leaving Home

As I lay in my bed, I gazed out the window and began to realize how beautiful the trees are, their stern branches with their green leaves. It was amazing to enjoy the nature that surrounded me. I had not really taken much notice before, but it was truly beautiful to enjoy what had already been here for so many decades.

Greenery has become a part of my life these days; although, it has always been a part of my life I didn't respect it as I do now. I guess to some it's silly to gaze at how beautiful Mother Nature is, but like many including myself, we are so busy with daily living that we just don't have time to appreciate the finer things in life. The sweet smell of the grass was something I never took notice of, and I never allowed myself to enjoy the beauty of its wholesomeness; nor, the relaxing realms of each blade. For some reason, we are always seeking enjoyment elsewhere by going on exotic vacations when Mother Nature's beauty is right in front of us. It's like having the wholesome Ivory girl right next door, and yet we don't notice her until she becomes a star. I constantly find myself at the window looking at flowers of many colors and shapes that surround the neighboring homes. They are exhilarating and pretty. I enjoy the sun now, it's not a nuisance or imaginary anymore. I enjoy the golden reflection as it beams through the windows. I can almost enjoy the heat that it projects. Also, the moon being born of many shapes, full, half, quarter shape, and so forth. They are all an inner part of my life now more than ever. I don't take anything for granted, anymore because now I realize these miraculous beauties can be taken away from me, and leave me without the joy of appreciating their beauty.

It was the year of 1990, in November, when I received a phone call from my Colonel, who informed me that the unit was pending alert; which means that the unit may be activated to go on active duty. I was new to the army, a second Lieutenant in the Army Nurse Corps Reserve, a "butter bar" as my father always called me. Meaning, officers that out ranked the enlisted were considered soft and received all the credit, while the enlisted did all the work. I knew the country was having problems in the Middle East, with Saddam Hussein, the leader of Iraq who had taken over Kuwait to regain control over the country and oil; however, I never gave that much thought of being called to serve; after all I was a nurse. And, I was aware that the current President, George Bush had already ordered many soldiers to the Middle East, including medical professionals; as early as August, so it wasn't a surprise that my unit was pending alert. When the final order came, I was in a state of shock. I didn't know what to think, or what to do, but I had this gut feeling that if we were to go, I would be one of many thousands. I tried to prepare myself mentally, but it was hard to do. I knew I had to tell my husband but I didn't know how. My husband was a male chauvinistic individual who believed women had their place, and that place was in the home. He was also egotistic and this situation might crush his ego, so I decided not to tell him until I was sure I would go.

The next morning I called the army to validate the call I had received last evening, it was true we were going to be deployed. I also learned that I was scheduled for Officer Basic School (a minimum requirement for all new officers entering the Nurse Corps.). I was scheduled for San Antonio, Texas; December 8, 1990 for two weeks. I couldn't believe it-I was finally going to officer school after serving for two years. I had been trying to go ever since I became commissioned. I had always been told there were no funds available, no slots, and besides my weight made it impossible each time I inquired. And, now the truth was staring me in the face, I was going to be deployed, overweight or not. A part of me was thrilled I was given this great opportunity to go overseas, something I had looked forward to in the army. However, I was not prepared to see lives destroyed by guns, bombs and chemical warfare; I was a nurse trained in my specialty. It didn't matter what I believed in if I was ordered, I had no other choice. I had sworn to save my country, I was obligated, and regardless of my beliefs I was a soldier.

That afternoon, when I told my husband what was going on, he didn't look surprised at all, and like myself he too expected it. He turned to me and said, "the media said they were calling thousands and thousands of reservists, and I felt that you would be called also." Although his voice sounded relaxed and prepared, he like most was afraid of the possibility of his spouse getting killed. Death never occurred to me then because I believed in the Father who was my protector and Supreme Being. I really didn't give death much thought. Besides, I believed I was going to heaven. I didn't know what to think or feel. One part of me felt strong, and obligated to the point that I allow myself to think I could handle anything, as long as I believe and stayed focused on the Lord. But then there was the other side of me that was afraid and didn't know how to express my fears. I knew what war could do, I had seen too many talk shows, and had taking care of too many post war veterans who suffered from post traumatic stress. I saw the devastation and the cruelty that war had caused so I too was frightened. I was frightened of what the war could do to me, but one thing I was certain of—I would miss my children terribly. I wondered how the war would affect my children, while I was so many miles away. I didn't want our relationship to change, but I knew deep in my soul that war would change me because war never left people the same. Despite my concern for my loved ones, I had a commitment and a duty to the country and fellow troops. I could not allow myself to become a coward. I was a soldier/nurse first, and a civilian second, so whatever skepticism I was feeling it didn't waiver my acceptance to go. Maybe that was the reason I had never given death much thought only because I wasn't afraid of dying. I knew that if I continued to trust my faith, death would pass me according to the word of God. I had come to terms with accepting death, but I did not want to die prematurely, while my children were still young and needed their mother; besides, I could not fathom anyone taking care of them except me. No one could raise them like I could and no one understood each of them like I did. And if anyone else would have that opportunity, no one would be capable other than my mother. My mother was already in her late middle age, and it would not have been fair to burden her with more responsibilities. That made me feel guilty, but it was a thought of so many thoughts I had to struggle with. I continued to maintain my focus on the positive, and I refused to allow myself to think on anything negative which could possibly hinder my obligations, commitment and loyalty to my country. I had allowed myself to understand the magnitude of it all, regardless of what anybody else thought or felt. The only regret I had was leaving my family, especially my daughter who was in her senior year in high school, ready to graduate and she needed me the most. I knew she would be fine, but I needed to give her the support. I was surely disappointed because I had already made plans to visit my parents in New York, and now my plans had to change. My children did not understand what was really occurring-they thought I was teasing. My daughter; on the other hand, was outraged. She couldn't believe it. She was too concerned and consumed with herself, her brothers and step-dad and she was not crazy about the idea of me leaving her. I really felt the pain she was feeling at the time, I was leaving a great deal of responsibility on her. As she and I talked, she explained that she was also afraid that she might never see me again. As we pondered thoughts of what the future might hold, we ended our conversation and I prepared to get ready for officer school.

I didn't know where to begin. I knew I had to take my military uniforms but I didn't know what to bring or leave behind because it was my first time. I was so frustrated over making this decision that I mentally became exhausted. I did know one thing for sure-I had to go to Fort Stewart to get the rest of my military attire. The drive was about an hour and a half long, and everything seemed so rushed when I arrived. I had so much to do in such little time. I found myself asking where to find the clothing store; as well as, the exchange. It wasn't that difficult; it just seems like it's forever when you don't know exactly where to go. After I located the departments I needed, I had to get my skirt tailored and fitted. The military had its restrictions on how your uniform must be worn and the last thing I needed was not to be in compliance. The seamstress was very friendly, and told me, "Although it's a short notice I think I can have these uniforms back to you within two hours." I could not argue with the time, after all, I lived too far to come back, so I decided to wait along with a friend who was with me which helped a lot because I suddenly found myself to be hungry. We went to find something to eat. We were so hungry we decided to stop off at Burger King; rather than, a restaurant because we were running out of choices and time. There was not a whole lot to do after we finished eating, so we drove around and enjoyed various sights, not that there were many. We stopped at a shopping plaza to buy a few extra items. And as time would predict it, we realized we were running out of time. Two hours had already passed and it was time to pick up my uniform. We drove back to the tailor shop where I had the privilege to try it on. It fitted very well I paid the lady, and we were on our way back to Jacksonville. The drive back was terrible because it started to rain and we could barely see the road ahead of us. As usual there were idiots on the road driving like they were in a car race. The rain didn't cease much, it began lightening and thundering, and at one point it seemed to fade away but once we passed certain areas the rain again began to pour. Finally, when we passed through Georgia the rain ceased and we were once again safe. It seemed like it took forever to get home.

When I arrived home I had so much to do. I packed the rest of my belongings and said my goodbyes to my children, since I would be gone for two weeks. My children always seemed to look so pitiful when I had to go away as if they knew more than I did. Their sadness; however, didn't surprise me since we were a close family and had always had a fear of goodbyes . . . at least I did. I finished packing my duffel bag and tried to retire for bed. I kissed my children good night and went into my room. My husband was at work and I would not see him until early the next morning. I lay in my bed wide-eyed and unable to sleep, anxious about my trip and my expectations. This was new to me. I remember thinking. It was not the flying that frightened me; it was the additional training that I would receive that would prepare me for the war. I didn't know what to expect, but I knew for sure that I was going to give it my all. Before I knew it, my husband was tugging my shoulder. I had over slept, and I did not hear my alarm clock. I awoke in a stupor only to find myself moving without much energy. I was trying to hurry but I just couldn't get my bearings together. I knew I had to make my flight but I was not fast enough, and the plane flew without me. I was so nervous I didn't know what to do; because all I kept thinking was that I was going to be in Texas, all-alone. Fortunately, I was able to reschedule and board the plane within one hour and to my surprise I reached San Antonio, Texas before the plane I had originally scheduled arrived. What a coincidence.

Chapter 2

Beginning Training

San Antonio was lovely. The airport was crowded as most airports are and the people seemed friendlier than what I was used to, or maybe it was my military attire the people respected. Whatever the reason I wasn't going to complain. We rushed on the crowded military bus that would take us to Ft. Sam Houston. Once we reached our destination we stood in long lines to process in, there must be something with lines in the military because I stood in many of them. There were so many lines, a line for this and a line for that. I can definitely understand the complaint of aching feet. Processing in took several hours. I was worn and tired. I wasn't hungry all I wanted was a shower and sleep. After processing was finished, we were briskly rushed again on military buses back to the hotel. The hotel was pretty and it sat on a hill. To my surprise we had to wait in another long line to get our rooms. I was sick of lines; luckily it didn't take as long, just very confusing. Thinking that I had finished the hardest task, guess what? I had to find my bags before I went to my room. Once I received my keys I had to share my room with someone else and to my surprise that someone was not a smoker but she agreed to share and tolerate my smoke. My roommate was quiet and I thought we would hit it off well; since like myself she too was new to the army; until I learned otherwise that she was a living nightmare. She started off being very nice, and I felt that was a good sign of forever friendship but later I learned she was callous, unfriendly, and cold-hearted. We would do practically everything together: wake each other in the morning, have breakfast, ride the bus together, and take our classes together, everything together! We would after a class walk together, exercise and talk intimately about our relationships together. Then all of a sudden our closeness began to take a turn for the worst. I knew she was new to the army and was having a hard time adjusting. Although I tried to give her words of encouragement; she didn't want to be there. I also tried to boost her morale by exercising since both of us could lose a few pounds. At first it seemed to be working well, but I would awaken early in the morning only to find her in progress already. It didn't seem to bother me at first, but this so-called buddy system was not working. I would find myself doing everything for her as if she was Ms. Nightingale; I practically waited on her hand and foot. I didn't allow her to dampen my mission since the motto was trained, trained, trained. I would arise early, as it is required in the military to attend long classes on how to be an officer and what to expect when we arrived in Saudi Arabia. There was so much to learn about military codes and their ethics that it was crammed in two weeks. Although it was tough trying to learn it all, I can say I became more educated than I was before. I would notice distance between us; she would wait until I went to sleep to exercise, and she would not wait for me on the bus anymore or save me a seat like she use to. I began to mingle with other officers, the ones that she talked about the most. I started to pay her little attention and she would pout like a six-year-old, but I didn't let her get to me. It was awful, I felt like a toddler and started to resent the immaturity we both were portraying. I couldn't believe I was acting so childish, here I was with three children of my own and I was behaving more immaturely than they. It was amazing, we were roommates, slept in the same room together and now we had become so distanced. It came a time when we didn't speak to each other. We continued to do our training as if we shared separate rooms. There wasn't any communications nor friendship left, I didn't think this friendship could be saved. It had become salvaged.

We had come to the end of our two weeks there, and everyone seemed excited and ready to go home. We had studied so much material and I'm not sure if we would retain it all. There were preparations being made for our party, pictures and our last days at the school that we hardly had time to do anything else. We did manage to go to the mall and visited various sites. Although I didn't get a chance to visit all the wonder attractions, I did manage to see the Alamo and the River Walk. Graduation would end our training. Time was inevitable and there were so many things happening. We were planning our party and all the excitement that went with it. The party was beautiful and not to my surprise, my roommate didn't show. I had a good time getting to know the rest of the officers and exchanging phone numbers in hopes of seeing them again when we have our reunion. After such a good time and enjoying the company of the brave I said my goodbyes and goodnights. You would not believe what happened! I had an idea that my roommate would pull some crazy stunt, but I didn't think she was so ruthless. I had prepared myself for the worst, so I called the front desk and requested a wake up call. I had prepared and packed most of my clothing earlier, except for what I was wearing home, I was ready. I was not going to be caught with my pants down at the cost of stupidity. Sleeping sound as she thought I would, my roommate awakened quietly in the midst of the night, hoping I would not hear her and began to dress. I was still not trying to let her know that I was aware of what she was doing, so I pretended as if I was asleep, but it was fine with me. I was prepared. My two weeks here had taught me survival skills. My roommate eventually left without saying a word. I slept a few minutes more before I began to get myself ready to return home.

 The flight was beautiful as usual and I was on time. When I arrived in Jacksonville, my husband was there, awaiting me. After exchanging greetings and hugs I went to retrieve my baggage. The lines were long as they normally are, so it took some time before I was able to receive mine, once I received my belongings we were on our way back home. Home was always the castle of my eyes; the emotions of closeness and concerns for one another were always the center of my heart. Something about family always brought goose bumps on my skin. I was glad to be home, but I knew it would only be for a short time. My unit had been activated and I was ordered to report to Fort Stewart in a few days. I was heart struck because Christmas was only a few days ahead and I wanted to be home with my family. Christmas had always been one of my favorite holidays; but now I was going to share this day with people I wasn't very close to. How could this happen? How insensitive could the military be to send me away from my family on our special day? They weren't all that insensitive; they did care about family togetherness I thought, they did allow me to enjoy the holiday with my family. But to my surprise the job was extremely short on staff and they needed me to work Christmas Eve so I did with the approval of my family. I was a workaholic anyway, and maybe I worked so I would not have to see the sadness in my families' eyes since I was going to be deployed in a few days. I wanted my priorities to be in the right perspective. I wanted to be assured that my family was secured when I departed, even if that meant, an additional paycheck. I could visualize myself as a child again; being the middle child with one brother and one sister. I was always the caregiver since my parents worked all day and most nights trying to provide a better life for my siblings and me. I wanted to do the same since I too have been indoctrinated to keep the family alive and well. Sometimes it was hard because I would find myself doing all the chores while my siblings enjoyed their social life. So yes, I choose to work to provide for my family, at least, I was assured that an additional paycheck would help them and not hinder them. I knew it would bring disharmony to my husband, but I knew in my heart I was doing the right thing. I was going away and I didn't know when I would return. My husband was supportive at times, but I felt he really didn't want me to go. He tried to convince me on things I could do to get out of it, but I wanted to be a part of the unit and that meant going to war with them.

    Christmas was beautiful; I was able to stay up most of the day and I didn't get a chance to sleep, since I worked all night. We exchanged gifts and my husband stayed up the night preparing our feast, which was very delicious. I was happy, but I knew this would be the last time we would be gathered soon as a family, for I would be gone for months or maybe a year. My children did not try to show their emotions as much, but you could see that they were tense, but my husband was the most tensed. I don't know if he was tense because I was leaving and he would have to play the role of being a father and mother and deep inside he didn't have a clue. There were so many unanswered questions and I was unable to find the answers. I can't tell you exactly what he was really thinking because I don't think I can honestly answer them, but I often wondered if he expected me to return home alive. My husband, you see, had the characteristic of a macho man and he believed a woman's place was in the home and I don't think he had enough confidence in me or for that matter the military system. His projection of the military was we were going to go over there and get killed. It's true some soldiers lost their lives and did suffer humility but I could not focus on death as he thought I should. I had confidence in my country then and I have confidence in my country now. Our conversation was always the focus on death and the what ifs and "why aren't you scared?" or "you should be crying." I was a strong woman, born from genes of a strong woman and man, with a sound spiritual knowledge that helped me feel confident. Christmas ended peacefully and my children were happy with the gifts they had received. We didn't talk much about my departure because I believe I would see them again before I was officially deployed. The next morning was crazy. I spent the most of it and mid-afternoon buying apparel and preparing myself of the things

I needed. I was busy and frustrated because I could not convince myself of what to bring. I knew (once I got there it wasn't too late to buy additional items if needed), the good thing about it, I would be on a military base. If I needed to get something I would still have some time before I left to go to Saudi Arabia.

Chapter 3

Training At The Mobilization Site

My unit was departing on the next day and I was sure that I had everything I needed to make my stay there more comfortable. I arrived at the unit about five o'clock. Familiar and unfamiliar faces that filled the parking lot surrounded me. There were loads of baggage everywhere and it was almost impossible not to bump into people as you passed them. This was our finale we were truly being activated it was real, and we were really going. We had our last formation at our unit. It was sad, crowds of families gather together to say their goodbyes most of them in tears. Flashes from the cameras nearly blind you as the flash sparkled in your eyes. There were so many people there including the television crew who also came to get news coverage. Our buses arrived and everyone began to exchange goodbyes to their loved ones. My husband looked so pitiful, as if he knew something I didn't know, but it was something I had gotten used to. I tried to stay strong because that's how I was taught to be. But, like everyone else I also found that I was unable to fight the tears. One thing that kept so many of us alive was that we knew once we arrived at Fort Stewart Ga. we would be able to see our families again, so there was still hope. Once I boarded the bus for some reason I felt a part of me was relieved, as if something had been released. I felt as if I was being let free but sad that I was leaving my children. I was unhappy in my marriage. My husband would show mixed feelings and send mixed messages, at times I really didn't know what to think but I knew I was unhappy and I really took this departure as a well-deserved one. You see I had just returned from San Antonio, Texas, and I had plenty of time to think of what I wanted in a marriage and for some reasons I was not getting all the love and support I needed. But as usual, my husband would give me all the reason why we should stay married and as always I would take the bait. There was this little person inside of me that wanted the marriage to work, but then I knew deep in my soul that it would never come to pass. I guess having Christ in your life you see things differently and you are hoping that he will change the things in your life that causes the most strife, but if all parties are not willing then Christ cannot operate. Life can truly be amazing; people see you and you're suffering inside but you cover up all the pain that is tormenting you with a smile, so for the most part, people believe what they see, but it's a lie. The bus door closed and the motor sounded and we were enroute to our mobilization site. Once the bus moved on we were able to regroup and think on things more pleasantly. We shared cookies, chatted some and laughed but deep down inside we were scared. We arrived at Fort Stewart Ga., and our gear was unloaded as we waited. The base looked almost ghost-like as if no one lived there. I guess being dark had a lot to do with it. We were assigned rooms in the barracks once we got our belongings. I didn't know at that time that I would share a room with but I was praying to God that it wasn't Ms. Nightingale again.

If you haven't been on a military base, I can assure you, you would know one immediately. The buildings always looked so historic and the barracks are always made of cemented materials as if the material had some magical protection against the enemy. This was my second home and I had to adjust as if I had no other choice, bedsides going AWOL. I knew this was only temporary and despite it all I would become a survival soldier with all the extensive training that was ahead of me, and I would be able to tell my story. The rooms were small and emptied: nothing but two beds, a dresser, nothing you could compare to your house or the Omni Hotel, it was definitely a place for sleep; the added comforts were what you brought. Of course there was a heater that sometimes worked, depending on how much power was being used. I shared the room with another soldier who was definitely not a household name and to many other officers she was a nightmare. She was different and unique in her right, but we got along swell. I fell in love with the barracks; I guess it grows on you after a while. We did have a pay phone in the barracks, but it was always being used, so the time you waited it was always better to use the phones outside. The only complaint I had was the bathroom, it only had three sinks, two toilets, and four shower stalls with no shower curtains that made it difficult when there were eight females who needed to use them. My solution to that problem was to arise early to enjoy the comfort of the bathroom alone. It was not always easy because I would have to get up early, but I needed the privacy. Formation was its usual rain or shine. You had to be there or you would definitely hear about it, and you didn't want the nonsense that went with it. Once formation was finished, we would board the buses for chow and as usual the officers had to eat last, (this was a military custom) once the enlisted were through. Chow was always good. You had so much variety to choose from. Transportation was limited and sometimes you had to skip a meal, but when I did get the chance to go I took advantaged of the selections. Although chow was delicious and I stuffed my stomach well, I did regret it later; it did show up again as unwanted pounds. This may account for the shortage of food in Saudi as rumors circulated but I wasn't the only one.

Chapter 4

Training, Training, Training

Scheduled training was posted and since I was in San Antonio, Texas, I had to make up all these classes the unit had already taken. Most people may assume that once a unit is called to war that they are automatic shipped on a plane or ship. But there are so many procedures involved: they include extensive training, medical work-up and dental evaluation, vaccinations, legal issues, and in-services about the country you are being deployed to, and you will not be deployed if you are not in 100% compliance with United States military regulations. It is not as simple as one might think; a lot of work goes into each soldier on an individual basis. The first thing I had to do was to process in. I had to see the doctor: get my whopping eight vaccines I needed to be deployed, take care of legal matters, initiate power of attorney for my family, and last get a green card. Believe it or not this took several days to do and once I was finished I was exhausted, since transportation was limited and the departments were so far from each other. It was unbelievable at times because if you didn't get a ride you had to call a military taxi and most of the times they were busy or they took forever to come. Although the frustration was over; I still had to see the dentist to be medically cleared and yes I took advantage of it, I smiled a lot better these days. By the end of the day I was tired and there was nothing left to do but make plans for another day, shower and go to sleep. This was my mobilization site. This was the group preparation before my departure; the army was making sure everything was in order before I left. This was good; it showed the military cared for its people and they were doing everything they knew to ensure everything went well. There were so many things to do and so little time to do it in, but it was being done day by day. I had to make another trip to the doctor, this time for my ingrown toenails, since I suffered so badly with them I didn't want anything to keep me back from going abroad. At first the doctor suggested I have them removed permanently, but if I did that I would have had to stay behind. I didn't want to be separated from my unit. I wanted to be there with my unit no matter what happened; I felt I was obligated to them. After all I had been with the unit for several years and I was part of them. I wanted to be with them, if it meant going to war with hurt feet. Although some of the soldiers suggested that this was my opportunity to stay in the states. I refused to take their suggestion seriously. I was bent on going and being a part of my unit; I decided to get my ingrown toenails done temporarily. The day of the outpatient surgery the doctor reiterated the procedure and stated I had made the right decision as with most surgeries, the risk of having them done temporarily or permanently was infection. The doctor was a female and although I thought that would make the pain less bearable; I realized it wouldn't have mattered what the gender was because the several needle sticks in my toe were worse than going through childbirth. The pain was excruciating; it was horrible. It was very, very painful. At one point I wanted to stop but it was too late. I couldn't turn back, so I continued clinching my teeth and biting into my lips until it was over. I don't think I would recommend this procedure to anyone. I think I will play doctor on my feet from here on. Don't get me wrong, the doctor was gentle, but nothing she could do to erase the pain of those needle sticks that gave no respect. I was given quarters (meaning no duties for whatever time the doctor indicated) pain medication and antibiotic ointment to apply to my feet for several days. I was also given permission not to wear my boots, which I hated anyway, but like most things nothing lasts forever. I was in too much pain to enjoy my leave and I was indeed hungry when quarters were completed. Although my meals had to be delivered, they forgot about me the first evening and I had to order pizza, which probably was a lot better. Quarters were finished, and I had to hobble around in discomfort to formation, scheduled training, and the chow hall. Of course the rumor was out that I wasn't going to Saudi Arabia but as with most rumors there is never any truth just idle gossip. I was not a coward I was determined to fight for my country no matter what people said as with most idle gossip the gossip came from idle thinking, and empty heads. Unlike myself, there were many that remained back for whatever reasons, some legitimate and some just, frankly scared. My painful feet lasted several more days and I was able to return to a steady gait in about a week. I wasn't completely healed and my feet didn't hurt as much. The good thing about having ingrown toenails removed was the outcome lasted approximately three to four months and I didn't have to worry about hurting feet for a while. A coward I certainly was not and besides I felt I owed it to my unit to be there with them no matter what the outcome. And no one knew the outcome or their destiny so it really didn't matter what people were talking; at least it didn't matter to me. All I knew I was going to defend my country and to take care of my soldiers who would get injured and I wasn't going to do anything to hinder my departure. Scheduled training went on as usual and supplies were issued and distributed. There were still so many things to do that sometimes it became unbearable and you felt as if you were never going to leave there. Family day was here and I was finally reunited with my family. The reunion went well and we decided to stay at one of the local hotels in town. Once we were together, we decided to have dinner, and would you know it would be Chinese food. We decided to make the evening special by ordering some wine and made toasts for the special occasion. Unfortunately, my husband would join the children and me later because he had to work, compliments from his job. Once my children and I finished dinner, we chatted for a while and went back to the hotel that was very much in walking distance but we drove anyway. We did manage to stop by the convenience store and fuel up on goodies that stretch our waistlines. Once we returned to the hotel I gave them their gifts I had purchased for them, they were elated. It seemed so improper to reunite this way, but we had decided to make the best out of it while I waited for my husband who would not be with us for some several hours, which seemed like forever. My children and I watched television and reminisced on happier moments, but we all knew it would be a matter of time before we would say goodbye for a long time. It was such a weird feeling I thought, "how was I going to adjust with them not being around me for some indefinite time". I really didn't know how I was going to handle it, but I knew I had to be strong for them. We tried very hard to forget about what was really happening but it was very difficult and much more difficult for me since I was the one who was having the pain with the eight vaccines shots I had received earlier that day which caused my concentration to become baffled. Sleep was not able to keep us bound no matter how hard we tried. I was as always the first one to fall asleep anyway. I showered, and put on something sexy for my husband when he arrived which was about six a.m. the next morning. I knew he was tired. But he as always tried to be more than he really was, even if it meant he was about to fall on his face he still would try to hang just to prove a point, something I never could understand. I tried to love him but time was inappropriate since the children weren't really sleeping and I didn't want to take any chances. I decided later on that morning to treat them to breakfast at one of their favorite restaurants, but they looked sad since I had to leave them. My husband and I were finally alone and we shared each other as if it was the first time. I wanted to be close to my husband and besides I was going to another world sort of speaking and I wanted to make amends. Time permitted us to be in ecstasy, but I was long over due in picking up the children, and the look on their faces showed disapproval when I arrived and how angry they were. I tried to make them happy by buying them some more gifts and that did make a difference. We continued to enjoy the afternoon but as always time was getting near and before we knew it I had to return back to the base. Once I returned back to the base, we had formation and as usual the officers always looked out of synch and out of place. I guess one of the reasons why we looked the way we did in comparison to the enlisted is because they are given more military knowledge during basic training (which last eight weeks) than we are. Our training as I have said before only lasted about two weeks. Usually you can tell the ones who have had prior service as a result of their training.

The next morning wasn't any different from the others; breakfast was as usual with the officers being last since there were not enough military buses to board us all. Once you did arrive to eat you still had to wait on long lines before you could eat and once you received your meal most of the times you had to rush your food down. The day continued as scheduled train, train, train!

I had to visit the legal office again since my husband convinced me that he needed the right document to take care of the children stating that the document that I first received was nothing. Me being a Christian, I decided to get general power of attorney. I felt if I wanted my marriage to work I had to establish trust somewhere; so, I decided to make him general of power of attorney, which would override my sister who had power of attorney, but the wills remained the same and my sister had control over that. After talking to a friend and fellow officer, which holds true today, she felt I had made a big mistake, but me having faith as I did, I never worried. I went to the exchange afterward to buy some items. I later returned to the barracks. I showered and fell asleep; I don't remember having chow, I guess I was too exhausted. I had a dentist appointment after formation so I hurried chow, which was not hard to do, and called a taxi.

During my visit the dentist suggested I have several teeth extracted, since he felt I was not deployable in the condition my teeth were in, that was all I needed was missing teeth in the front of my mouth. The dentist recommended repairing it, but the only problem I had against me was time? "Can all this work be done before my departure" I thought. Well, it was. Extraction of the teeth was done, antibiotics and anti-inflammatory medicine was given and I received my new look in four days. The wait and pain were well worth it. My smile was essential to me; my self-esteem did not need to be shattered.

Troops were becoming anxious toward our departure date, but no one had a clue when we were going to leave, they only speculated from idled gossips and rumors. The days began to seem longer and the soldiers were becoming impatience, they wanted to perform their mission and they wanted to leave as soon as possible. Then they became more upset, rumors had it that the unit was over strength, and some soldiers might have to be left behind and sent to other units that needed their expertise. The nurses were not excluded. The chief nurse had also stated that she had too many nurses, which she called excess. So daily, army nurses would go to the bulletin to see if their names appeared on the list. This was frustrating to those who wanted to share the overseas experience like my roommate and me. My roommate was having a hard time getting along with the chief nurse, she was sure she would be excess baggage (meaning, she would be an additional nurse, not needed, and would not be able to deploy with the unit) and her dream unfulfilled if the chief nurse had anything to do with it. I tried to console my roommate, but nothing I said had any comfort at that time. Then there were the cowards. The always ready soldier, but when it came time for them to defend their country, all sorts of aliments became prominent: like heart problems, lung problems and anything they could think of to relieve them of going over seas.

For some of the soldiers, some were relieved of going overseas they got to stay in the states and for some their world was crumbled because they were ordered to be attached to other units. The rest of the day was spent doing physical fitness, attending in-services and extensive training. I knew the time was near toward departure because my final task was to complete the gas chamber's exercise, but my intention was to be with my family without permission, and that is exactly what a fellow soldier and I decided to do. I called my husband and asked if he could come and get us, and he didn't hesitate. I felt sorry for him than I did myself, since he had not seen his wife for a long time because of finances and not having a car. I was bored myself and his could not have come at a better time, so I opt for the chance and at the same time made someone happy. If you could have seen the look on his wife's face you would have done the same thing, it was a look I will never forget. Unfortunately, our night didn't last too long, before I knew, it was time to return to the base without getting caught. We arrived at the mobilization site early and rushed to make it to formation on time, once I arrived there, I noticed some unhappy faces. Rumors had it that a list was circulating and the names on that list were not going to be deployed with the unit. The excess (people who were not deploying with the unit) list really didn't bother me at first; because I knew I was not the fortunate one, but I did have sad a feeling of not wanting to be separated from my friends, besides we needed each other. For once the rumor held true, and my name did not appear on the roster. The names that did appear showed the uncertainty on their faces. Some were disappointed but for others you could see right through them that they didn't care at all. The sad thing about it the ones that did want to go were cast away like a foreign throw away. They were feeling betrayed. My roommate was included in the excess, and she felt and looked awful that she would not have this great experience to share. She was angry and felt this was done to her deliberately. I was lost for words, I did not know what words to say to her or how to comfort her in her time of despair, and she knew that too.

    The next morning sick call was overcrowded. There were so many soldiers there trying to find an aliment to get out of this completely. Most of my buddies were not going with me and I didn't know where they would be located, I kept reminding myself that wherever they would be, I hoped they would be safe. Time was essence we were moving fast, our training at Fort Stewart had been completed, and we were well on our way to our new destination. I was not moved or afraid, I had God in my life and he helped me to feel secure. I prayed daily. Our last days were getting more supplies, packing, and rearranging. We were told we are allowed to carry one duffel bag and a rucksack. Of course this was a traumatic experience for me so I did what I was told to do, follow orders. The unit was ready. We were motivated and ready to do our mission. The last few days at our mobilization site we carried on as usual, arising at the break of dawn, attending formation and performing our last minute trained activities. The unit on a whole was motivated to get the job done and support our country, we had prior knowledge of what to expect, it was just a matter of the troops getting there and putting what we learned in place. The days seemed as if they were becoming longer and the nights seemed to last the longest. The count down had begun and you could see the anticipation on the soldier's faces asking, "what if?" I was ready to go and support my fellow troops, and get this over with.

    Later that day, I decided to call my family who was happy to hear from me and expressed how they missed me terribly. My children told me that they prayed daily for the war to end so I would be able to come home. I felt guilty because one part of me yearned to be there and yet a part of me wanted to be with my family. I wanted to be there for my own experience, not just as a female but as an American. I wanted to go, so it was difficult for me to express my true feelings, because I didn't want my family to think that I didn't want to be with them; they would have thought I was crazy to want to be a part of a war where killings took place. However, it was not the killing that excited me. It was the American way of getting the job done and doing the right thing to defend the country. Or maybe it was the adrenaline that increases every time I thought about how many lives I would be saving or how many wounds I would bandage; maybe, it was the rush I felt of doing something that many millions didn't have the opportunity to do. Maybe, I felt special or unique because I was going to assist in a good cause. Although I have never given death much thought, I was willing to die for my fellow man; I was willing. I think my husband thought I was being ridiculous, but on the other hand I might have been called a feminist, but the thoughts of so many really didn't matter to me, what really matter was how I felt and what I believed. My husband would have appreciated it if I had been crying, complaining or scheming on how to get out of not going to war, but the more he tried to persuade me, the more I wanted to go; besides I felt compelled to give something back to the men and women who lost their lives in Vietnam who had no choice. They were the men who could not escape the jungles of death, what made me any different because I was a female, a wife and a mother; most of those men were boys the many few who had just celebrated their eighteenth birthday. If I had an advantage over them, I was almost twice their age, and if my life at that time had a destiny for death then my age had an edge on them. Time was winding down; we had only two days left before we would be on our way to the Saudi Desert. My last few days were overwhelming. I spent the last moments with last minute packing and saying goodbyes.

Chapter 5

The Plunge Or The Beginning

The day of departure was finally here. We were up earlier than our usual time trying to see who was going to get to shower first. When I finished showering, I brought my bags to the front to be loaded in the five tons. It was chaotic, there was no organization as usual, the dark sky did not make it any helpful, soldiers and bags were everywhere. Soldiers were gathered around trying to load their belongings on the five ton trucks. I cannot tell you how anxious they were, it seemed as though some were becoming a little pushy, not to mention a little angry. I guess I would have felt the same way if I had to go back and repack my things after I had stayed up practically the whole night. The reason for this is because some soldiers had more than the allotted baggage that was allowed. This really caused more frustrations; because some of them had to leave some of their things behind. My belongings were loaded and I guess I was lucky to have my things on the truck without having to repack as so many others did. The dawn began to surface and it became brighter as if there was never any darkness. Many of us gathered around as if we had something to do, but there was nothing left to do but wait. Families greeted some of the soldiers while some of the others did various things like trying to get their belongings loaded on the truck.

A formation was called once everything was loaded and we were given a briefing of what to expect and the do's and don'ts, if that was any kind of consolation to allay some of our fears if we had any. All I wanted to do was to see this truck start rolling since I was not going to have the opportunity to see my family before my departure. It was really happening we were leaving today, the anticipation on faces were unreal, everyone looked so gloomy, but yet willing to do their jobs. I too was feeling sad for this was the finale, there was no turning back. Some of the soldiers that were attached to the hospital who were friends of mine were not going to make this trip. I know I would miss them as well. Most of all, they were not going to be there with me to share the experiences and I felt that was important and probably something to look forward to.

The buses were here and it was countdown time, as we stood in line to board them. Families were saying their good-byes as their loves ones boarded the bus. Some held on to their love ones as if they didn't want to let them go and you could see the tears on so many faces as we climbed the steps to take our places on the seats that awaited us. I fought back the tears that seemed inevitable, but they came anyway I wandered until I found a seat near a window next to a Lieutenant who was newly assigned to our unit. As the bus doors closed, the engine began to idle, and I knew then, we were on our way. As I looked through the glass windows I could see the teary eyed people as the bus poked along until we were no longer able to see any of them in sight; I began to cry once more. The Lieutenant tried to comfort me but that was something I needed to do. The tears didn't last too long and before I knew it I was enjoying the company of a disciplined Lieutenant. He was physically fit and his entire conversation was staying fit and passing physical training, which meant APFT (Army Physical Fitness Test). That was something I really wanted to hear about this time, when I missed my children and was on my way to a war.

I knew exactly what they were feeling. I also looked back to the site that seemed home for me for a while, having to let go so that I could venture to a new home, Saudi Arabia. Although it wasn't my real home, it would be my new home away from home, one way or another I had to adjust. Leaving Fort Stewart was a beginning of a new journey of uncertainty. Our next stop would be the Air Force base; the holding station where we would stay until our plane arrived. Uncle Sam was good to us. We had plenty of snacks, assorted sandwiches and coffee and tea, they knew we would probably not see American food for a while. Some of us who were not hungry grabbed cots, refreshed ourselves, and tried to get comfortable before our departure. I spent my duration eating, relaxing, reading and calling home; to my surprise my family was in North Carolina, so I left a message for them with the hotel clerk. I was a little disappointed because I wanted to speak with my children before the plane arrived because I didn't know how long it would be before I had the chance speak to them again. The holding place was a big place as if we were top secret, caged in with armed soldiers; I guess in a way we were top secret because we were going to war. I tried not to think of anything that would make me sad so I continued to chat with others as if everything was alright trying to pass time. A reporter from the unit was there and filmed us on video and anybody else who wanted to say hello and last minute goodbyes to their families. I have never seen the film nor do I believe my family has. Although it was a good idea, I must say it did relieve us from the separation pains we were having. The anticipation of waiting was great, it seemed forever but time always had a way of going slow when you needed it to run quicker, but as many others did I tried to make the best of it. I went outside to enjoy some last minute free air when I saw a soldier from afar crying. I went over to comfort her and she expressed she missed her baby that she had recently had along with her husband and other little girl. I felt her sadness and tried comforting her but what could I really say to a mother who had that motherly bond with her family, that was inseparable, but I expressed some reassurance that was so desperately needed and embraced her. She was so despondent with the separation that I detected she was angry, not at me but I guess with the whole situation, I could not blame her frustration and anxiousness because I too was somewhat in the same situation, who wouldn't be. Maybe I was repressing my feelings or truly had accepted the situation or just simply was in a state of denial, all I wanted to remember was what I was instructed and trained to do. All I wanted was to assist my troops, complete my mission and return to my family unharmed. The Chaplain came over and gave the young soldier some spiritual support and with the help of both our supports she was able to dry her tears from her eyes and move on. The Chaplain was a unique person he was always around to give a hand, say a prayer or express some kind words. There was something special about him, his love for Christ showed. There were a lot of sighs and talking as our plane arrived; I immediately got this feeling of a hot sensation and felt like butterflies were in my stomach. This time it was the real thing. There would be: no holding station, no mobilization site, no warehouse, I was going to Saudi Arabia, and that was about to happen. We all folded our cots, refreshed and waited in line to receive water and various items from a generous Red Cross representative; they were also there to see us off. We stood in line waiting to board the plane when a voice echoed instructing those who smoke to come forward so they would be seated first at the back of the plane. At first I was too embarrassed to raise my hand because there weren't too many smokers but since I was to sit with a Sergeant who smoked, it was only fair of the embarrassment. We boarded the plane and found our seats and I sat near the window. I was always fascinated to sit near the window and if we were hijacked or if the plane crash at least I may have the chance to go quickly, for some strange reason I thought. The soldiers continued to board the plane and I was able to place my belongings overhead during the chaos. I managed to weave myself through the crowd to visit the girl's room and to my surprise I quickly discovered I had a urinary tract infection, not because I was a nurse but because the symptoms were so painful any non-medical person would have known. One thing I knew for sure, I was going to hold my water for as long as I could. When I returned to my seat a male Sergeant occupied it, he felt he deserved it better, and before the plane could take off they were embraced in each other arms, kissing, necking and loving every minute of each other. It was hard not to see them since they didn't try to cover and I sat right behind them. It really did surprise me since this male soldier, just a few hours ago tried to talk romance to me. Not to mention he dated my girlfriend last year during annual training, and the simple fact remains he was married, and he didn't waste any time to allow the plane to leave the ground. While they continued in their romance interlude I conversed with a good buddy of mine, while I munched on a sandwich, who sat next to me the entire trip. The plane was ready for take off while the stewardesses made their appearance and thanked us for our courage and how they appreciated our bravery and what we were doing. The seat belts signal lights came on and we were ready for take off except it wasn't going to happen as planned; the plane was overloaded and some of the bags had to be removed and shipped later. I assumed the problem was taken care of since we took off into the sky and eventually out of sight to those who saw us off. If you haven't had the experience of flying, it is a great feeling and once the plane has reached its correct altitude you don't even know your feet are (several thousand miles into space); however, I must admit there are times when you go through turbulence and it is felt. I immediately put on my headphones when it was safe to do so and was soothed by good music. After a while I discovered I had to visit the girl's room again. I almost forced myself not to but nature was at its best and I had no control of it, the problem was becoming increasingly worse, so I saw the doctor that was aboard, and told him my troubles and he gave me some antibiotics that would solve my distress. It was hard for me to sleep so I watched others as they did and wondered what the future had in store for my fellow troops and me. Our first stop was New York, but we were not allowed to get off the plane and what better reason not to get off the plane since this was my hometown; however, we were allowed to stretch if that made much difference, while they fuel the plane. I wished I had told my parents to meet me here, I thought, but, that would have been some surprise, but I guess it was just wishful thinking. It was just a matter of a few minutes before we were on our way again and I continued to observe the rest of the crew while some slept, while others talked and some of them just looked dazed. Somehow I managed to get some sleep myself and awaken with aching and swollen feet, so I decided to take my combat boots off to give my feet some rest and air, to my amazement that was a big mistake because it was hell putting them back on. I must have slept a good while because it was dawn when I did awake. I think there was something wrong with those stewardesses because; every time I looked around they were feeding us, it seemed like we ate about every hour, maybe it wasn't exactly every hour but it sure seemed like it. The flight was beginning to make me restless and the cure for that was for me to sleep so I did exactly that and when the stewardess came around my hunger needs were met as well. Once again we stopped to fuel the plane and this time I believe it was Italy and to our surprise we received a new set of stewardess who spoke with beautiful accents. After the stewardess settled in and gave their welcome and safety briefing we were on our way again. I became restless and what better thing to do is sleep and that is what I did again. It seemed like forever but we were now in the skies of Saudi Arabia, it had been about 22 to 23 hours above the clouds and we had finally, without question arrived.

Chapter 6

The Landing, War Or Defeat

The weather was terrible, it was foggy and the fierce rain was making it impossible for the pilot to land. The pilot circled trying to avoid anything that might put us at risk but was having a hard time, so he decided several attempts to no avail. This scared the heck out of me because we had come too far to end up as casualties. After three attempts the pilot was able to land without difficulty. As I watched through the window, I realized the weather was awful; it was hard to see anything. The country looked like a ghost town; it looked as if there was no life at all. Recalling back to this day, I don't think we landed at the right airport. The weather remained horrible and the rain poured as if there was no intention of stopping and it was hard for us to see ahead. The rain felt like someone was standing there slapping your face. What could be better than our platoon leader deciding to call a formation (where the troops line up to be accounted for) at this time. I thought this was ridiculous since the rain continued to drench us without proper gear (protective rain clothing). However, this was only the beginning of chaotic leadership who out ranked us and exerted their power to direct. Until we received further notice we had to stand at ease until we were ordered to do otherwise, while standing in the rain. Thank God, I wasn't the only one who felt preposterous, to a command so facetious. We finally got the okay to move which required us to walk approximately one and a half miles to shelter. We walked through muddy waters while some of our belongings dropped from the plastic bags because they were soaking wet; we also lost many bottles of water. Our destination seemed like we were never going to reach it while the muddy waters made it hard for us to step through it comfortably. I didn't mind losing the bottle of water or MRE (meal ready to eat), which are sometimes referred to as Utopia foods; full of calories, dehydrated processed foods that make you feel like an orphan when you eat them; not to mention you can't move your bowels for several weeks. All I wanted was refuge and a rest room, unfortunately my idea of a refuge and a rest area was beyond anything I could imagine. However we did find sanctuary in a darkened huge room, filled with cracks and puddles of muddy water and rain that was seeping through the crevices. I didn't want to be indifferent and show frustrations so I adjusted like most of them, but I could not believe we stayed there for so many hours, not hearing from the advance party who was supposed to rescue us.

We were instructed to make ourselves comfortable for whatever that was worth and that was exactly what we did, some of us took our blankets and wrapped ourselves in them while others stood and chatted to each other. I decided to make myself comfortable by finding a place to rest my weary body despite the mud and all since I didn't know when we would get out of there, trying to make good of a bad situation. We stayed there for many hours and my uniform with many others was a muddy mess. We were finally leaving our sanctuary and there were four buses outside that greeted us and Palestinian men who were our designated drivers. These men were friendly as they greeted us; they were small in stature and had no muscular physique. They spoke broken English and their teeth were discolored and decayed; nevertheless, we were entrusted to them to take us to the advance party. The buses were small and the seats were built for people who were approximately about four feet, so we had to make the best of it. It didn't matter as long as we reached our destination in one piece I was thinking, and I wanted to be able to reach some clean water so I could take a shower and change into a clean uniform. The ride was so uncomfortable, TA 50 (army equipment) was everywhere including all the necessities the soldiers brought with them, the aisles were filled with baggage and anything you could think of. I began to feel hungry but I refused to eat MRE's (army package food rations), so I drank from my canteen that was only filled with water. We traveled across roads that were empty and desolated, bumpy and grounded with plenty of sand. Our ride was not a short one and we found ourselves lost in the desert, it was frustrating; since we were cramped, hungry and dirty, it's a good thing we did not smell yet. We drove around Saudi's sand for hours until we found the rest of the unit. I was certainly relieved when I was able to recognize familiar faces and smiles. From the scattered noises I wasn't the only one relieved they too were happy to see us as well.

Chapter 7

In Saudi

The area was located on a huge port, owned and name King Fahd, he must have owned millions because the port spoke for itself, with huge ships and everything that was needed to make it work. On this port there was this big warehouse that sat almost in the middle of the warehouse. As we arrived, we were told to get some cots, eat our MRE's and drink plenty of water, but thank goodness there was a food vendor that was a quarter of a mile that sold hamburgers and hot dogs the American way, and that is exactly where most went to feast. The hamburgers were a long way from McDonalds, but it beat MRE's any day. The warehouse was clustered and noisy with hundreds of soldiers and much chatter. It was hard to really get comfortable. There were so many things taking place, getting cots and waiting for our duffel bags, although it wouldn't take me long to find mine since it had a bright orange tag on it. Once I found where I would be residing and began to arrange my belongings the chief nurse decided she wanted to see the officers and enlisted separated. Although many felt this was a good idea, some found it ridiculous since bullets had no name whether you were an officer or an enlisted. This was the military and you basically did what you were told to do, it was an order and that's the way it went. With much sigh and frustration everyone rearranged themselves and their belongings so the separation of rank was completed. The warehouse was extremely large, there was nothing spectacular about it, and it was the typical warehouse. Our advance party had arrived earlier so they were able to set up a supply area, and signal area and had designated areas we had needed. Our unit was big, and we were not the only unit housed in the warehouse.

There must have been approximately a thousand soldiers that were housed in the warehouse. In the back of the warehouse was a small staircase that leads to the room of the chief nurse, and where other colonels slept. In the front of the warehouse near the supply area housed the commander, and that was where most of the private briefings were held. Because there were so many soldiers in the area the space between the cots were not even arms lengths, just enough room to put your duffel bag on the side of them. My one-foot cubic area was all I needed to place my family picture taped to my duffel bag above my head and a place to put the rest of my belongings. I guess I could call it the holding place or refuge, because many soldiers came and went. Outside the warehouse about a quarter of a mile were man made showers, they were a long way from home, but at least they provided some comfort and privacy for many. Adjacent to the warehouse were two latrines, one female and one male. The male latrine was made that half of the wood stood halfway and the rest was covered with see through screening, allowing people to see their faces and their chest, which sparked many giggles. The female latrine were very private, it consisted of four toilet covers and below were rusted big cans that acted as the receivers, in between one of the toilets was a stray ashtray that was compassionately left, rolls of toilet tissues were hooked on nails or placed on the shelf of the window. The bathroom had no lights so it was wise to bring your flashlight especially after the sun went down or you could find yourself sitting on a pile of waste or something within that realm. I'm not at all exaggerating that was the way it was, and you soon learned that some folks had no clue of cleanliness. It was a great thing we had the Palestinians to clean them daily, but this was home for now and we had to be mindful of others. We had to learn to adjust and make the best of it or our life there would be miserable, for this was only the beginning. The showers were pretty much similar to the latrines closed space and about 10 feet from the male and female showers but privacy between the sexes was utilized to the fullest. The shower water was cold but tolerable and I quickly discovered the best time to take a shower was when the sun was at its peak, when it beamed directly on the shower stalls' roof, this allowed the water to reach a warm temperature which enabled me to enjoy my shower much more, but I would learn to build a tolerance for the cold water as well. We were giving a briefing not to drink the water but it felt so good to swish the water in your mouth, like home. Later I was informed the water was baptized with bleach and Saudi's chemicals. Showers were on a time limit because as always there is always someone who abused the privilege, which allowed most of us to hurry when we used them. Directly in front of the warehouse docked a big ship, the port was huge there was so many of us, all you could see was army green camouflage.

Our first few days were lazy days we did absolutely nothing, and we did exactly that; however, one thing didn't change, we still had to form formations at the Commander's request, although it was at times hectic, it was to assure 100% accountability, that all soldiers were where they were suppose to be.

As time went on, I noticed constant meetings with the Commander and faces of frustrations on the other leaders in charge. As the meetings continued the face of the Commander in charge, looked apple red as if they were having major disagreements. I continued to watch with a keen eye but not allowing it to get the best of me, because whatever was happening I was sure the decision would be in the interest of the troops. My daily affirmation was listening to CNN, writing home, reading the Bible and keeping a journal. The troops were getting anxious; the word was out that the ground war would be starting on January 15, 1991. Some of the troops were upset and some of them were outraged, because this was Dr.Martin Luther King's birthday; and why would the government want to start war on that day when a man lost his life because he represented peace. I understood the feelings of the troops if you understand the philosophy of Dr. King. The CNN (Continental Network News) became my daily focus; it was like I was addicted to this station just as those who are addicted to soap operas. It was a ritual, I looked forward to viewing it, they kept me informed of what was going on and what Saddam was doing which seemed to be missed during our Formations and briefings. Although ground war was near, no one was giving any concrete information, it seemed as though everything we asked was answered invasively. One thing I did find out was whether we were being briefed or not, ground war was definitely near and CNN made that clear. But in truth no one was really sure, except higher headquarters. It became a guessing game for us; but one thing I did know, we had to be ready whenever it did happen. Because of this, CNN became my way of dealing with the pressures of Saudi and the not knowing. Sometimes I would lie in my bed at night trying to understand the complexities of a mind like Saddam Hussein who was filled with turmoil and the extreme measures he would go to, to gain control and power. I thought, what would make a person go to war knowing they would lose, how could anyone be so foolish? Although we were in his part of the land many thousands miles away, I felt no repercussion would befall us, I knew we would defeat him, but at what expense would it cost us. We were the power country, the land of wealth and prosperity, we were AMERICANS. There were so many questions racing through my head that I began to rationalize and make sense out of questions that really didn't have an answer or for that matter no validity. I had too many questions and no answers for most of them, and to this day some of them have not been answered. Something didn't seem fair in life, us being here and not knowing the real reason why we were there, but then again it didn't seem fair for the lost lives that served in the Vietnam War, but they were there too. I decided to go to sleep I had mentally beaten myself enough and I wasn't getting anywhere but becoming somewhat frustrated. Before I decided to go to sleep, I would write in my journal of the daily happenings, but never did I think I would transform the journal into a book. Morning was its usual sleepy eyes, frustrated faces and a race to the latrines, and last and not least the daily ritual of formation. Well, not everyone thought it was a great idea to get up at 6:00 a.m. for breakfast, especially the many that slept later. Most of us looked forward to breakfast for it gave us something to do, besides full stomachs, it really didn't matter to me, the only thing I looked forward to was a cup of hot tea, a buttered roll and a cigarette. Breakfast was always noisy and I always wondered how the rest of the late sleepers could stand it, because most of the activities took place in back of the warehouse, but they did, although today it was quiet and organized.

For the first few days we had MRE's and later given the honors of catered food by King Fahd. Although it was nothing like moms special it was well worth it and appreciated. The eggs were actually green "no kidding" they were, and their version of cold milk always seemed lukewarm, but it was far better than eating MRE's.

We were still given freedom to do what we wanted as long as it was constructive and that meant washing clothes, writing home and just plain relaxing, allowing our bodies a chance to rest. The time off was good, it gave me the opportunity to relax, write home, and read my Bible. It also gave me the opportunity to explore my surroundings, the port. There were big ships everywhere along with military equipment parked everywhere as well. There really wasn't a whole lot to do, since we were isolated and confined to the entire area mainly due to safety. Sometimes I would take two showers a day and sometimes it was just impossible to have any, since other troops were allowed to use them also. I had also found a way to make my life a little easier by washing my undergarments in the shower. It was certainly convenient than trying to find space by the wash area. This had imposed a problem to some since there were other units who participated as well. The only time I would use it if I needed to wash my BDU's, since that required dedication and much time. Although the idea of having clean BDU's were a must we soon discovered there was someone else who had the same interest but didn't want to put forth the effort or the time, many soldiers clothing became history, stolen. It was rare to have this happen but as usual it only takes one bad person to spoil the fun or privileges, yet many people continued to wash and hang their clothing at their own risk. Despite all the negative that was happening, something good was also happening as well, we received a new food vendor that arrived promptly everyday, and it was war. The food was free, compliments from the Army; but nothing compared to McDonald's or Burger King, but far better than what we were receiving from the Palestinians.

 The days seemed longer and I was beginning to feel them and it seemed as though we were stuck into a time zone, and nothing was happening. The same ole ritual became old. I found myself feeling as if I was held a hostage; I felt as if I was a captive and was in prison, and I had no way out, I felt smoldered, but I knew I had to adjust if I wanted my tour to run smooth. I was not the only one feeling that way after chatting with my fellow officers and enlisted troops they were feeling the same way as well. We all wanted something to happen, the wait was becoming too long, not because we wanted bodily harm or anyone hurt we just wanted to do our mission and get home to our families. The female Chaplain started a Bible study class and a chorus group that met in the evenings, this was great, and it gave us something to look forward to and another way of relieving our stress and getting our minds off what was to come and going home.

Chapter 8

The Desolate

Although the wait was taking its toll on some of the troops they continued to have a positive attitude and did whatever was needed to pass the time constructively. The chief nurse and others decided it would be very helpful to initiate sick call for the soldiers in the immediate area. This structure was organized in teams; nurses and enlisted troops, known as (ninety-one charleys). We worked various shifts to allow others to get the much needed rest. This was good; it allowed us to treat various units as well as our own from the common cold, injured eyes and suturing of simple lacerations. Although the gesture was good it didn't last long.

Morning came and we had the opportunity to go into town to shop and to make some phone calls if we wish. The only catch was you had to wear full MOPP gear, LBE and mask. All who wanted to go jumped on the five-ton (a large army truck) and found their places; it really didn't matter as long as we were off the port. The ride seemed endlessly long, tiring, and what would be better than to get lost, which we did. Asking directions was like asking a dead man to speak. We drove around town trying to find our way, but we were having no luck, and darkness was approaching. The driver turned a corner and discovered a Baskin Robbins Ice Cream Parlor; we thought we had hit jack pot when all of a sudden we saw a beam of light looking like an oversized bullet slowly flying in our direction overhead. Someone panicky yelled out MOPP 3; and everyone started to hustle for their protective gear in an attempt to be safe. It was unbelievable this was happening, but it was, I saw, it with my own eyes. I cannot express the palpitation of my heart, nor can I erase that it never happen. I was speechless and I was in awe. A scud missile had just passed over our heads, and although it looked like it was going slow it was actually going fast and could only to be intercepted by a patriot missile. A loud noise erupted and you could see the scud missile disperse into pieces. The question of trying to get to the phones was out of the question; our only concern was to get back to the warehouse. We drove through several traffic lights until it was safe to unmask, but most of us were afraid to take it off; and the ones who did take their masks off you could see the fright on their faces. When we arrived back to the port we couldn't wait to tell our stories and everyone listened as if they already had known, but was giving us a chance to vent our feelings. A cigarette was definitely in order and I couldn't wait to inhale and exhale to relieve some of my anxiety. I must confess I wasn't really scared, but it did give me confirmation that I was there. I had missed dinner so I had to find something else to eat, but what I wanted more than anything else was a shower and that was out. I settled with taking a quick cowboy something I had become all too familiar with and went to bed falling asleep between a scripture or CNN; maybe both.

Morning could not come fast enough, I thought, if I could see another day my days here would be shorter, but this was only a thought, and the beginning of many long days to come. I was restless and could not sleep. I prayed silently to myself in hopes of falling asleep, but it was not working I passed the guards and I visited the restroom.

Morning eventually did come, and as usual everyone completed their daily rituals as they did most of the mornings, except there were always a few who didn't believe in cleaning themselves before chow. Breakfast which was usually one of my favorites was beginning to get boring as well. The same menu over and over; green eggs, no ham, cold toast and rolls, warm milk and bitter coffee, but it was still better than MRE's or maybe I was just complaining.

The weather was hot, extremely hotter in the mid afternoon. As I gathered talking to some friends a truck with two Palestinians pulled up selling foods, drinks and BB's. I thought what the heck was BB's after a brief in-service giving by the two sergeants, I was convinced these finger rolled tiny tobacco brown cigarettes resembled marijuana joints and was substitution.

They smelled awful, but were the number one seller; although I had no plans in smoking them I was eager to have a pack as a souvenir. It seemed as though those who smoked them had the giggles. It was lunchtime and that meant going to the vendor over eating MRE's, if you were lucky like some others and like myself you had food stored away for days like this.

Gossip was flowing of our having to move to a new location, but it was supposed to be kept secret; however, nothing else was kept a secret; there was always somebody who couldn't keep his or her mouth closed. The war was beginning to take its' toll, the commander was becoming pale and thin. His face showed years of frustrations and his smoking had increased, although that may have been hard to tell since he always had a cigarette in his mouth or hand. He looked confused, weary and distant, there must have been some confusion about things he wanted to share, but he tried to keep a positive composure as if no one would noticed him.

Desert Shield was starting to show itself as the top brass hurled back and forth to meetings while we troops carried on as our usual. It was a couple of hours after dinner and the female sergeant who had deserted me on the plane to be with her male lover had asked me to accompany her to smoke a cigarette, and I did. The two of us stood outside the warehouse in a space that had become common for smokers to go to, as we chatted about any and everything; halfway through our cigarettes a familiar flair of light beamed over our heads. Suddenly a loud noise sounded as if an earthquake was taking place; and within a matter of seconds sirens began to screech across the port, and troops hysterically were running to safety. I was amaze and dumbfounded and quickly rushed inside the port for cover. It was chaotic, voices echoed in multitude to MOPP 4. It was a mess, everyone was hysterical and most of them didn't know what was exactly going on, just doing what was told and by following others. Friends who knew each other hurled together in groups, until we were told all clear, we did not know at the time, but soon discovered this was only the beginning of many sleepless nights that would take place frequently and haunt us forever; caused by a sick mind that had decided to prey on us, but this was war. I couldn't help at that moment to give God a silent prayer to thank Him, God had spared my life; we were standing right there when it flew across our heads and was intercepted by a patriot. All I wanted to do was sleep, going home was not a thought at that time, but one thing for sure my protective suit would become handy for now on. We were given anti-nerve-agent pills (pyridostygmine bromide) to counteract any untold affect we would have if we were attacked by nerve gas. They were not to be experimental, but it was not FDA approved yet; we were in the army and what they told us to do we believed and did. If this pill would help if such an attack did happen then we had agreed to honor the order. They were given in little paper cases and we were told to take them every eight hours. There were times we were reminded to take them. I wasn't sure if they worked or not, I just wanted to be safe if the situation arose. One thing I did noticed I had become constipated after I started taking them and had never developed dry mouth before; there were others who had the same symptoms.

While listening to CNN they had begun to broadcast about the attack I had just witnessed; they went on to say scud missiles were being intercepted everywhere. I could only think that Saddam Hussein was pretty upset by now, he was being beaten by his own game. Because there was so much chaos with downing the MOPP gear the Captain decided to give us a briefing that evening. There was a mix up on how to get fully mopped; because several people were giving directions instead of one person; which definitely caused the troops to get confused. Once the briefing was finished the Chaplain ended with a prayer and some positive words. As we headed back to our cots a friend started to ramble about how she had missed her children and she thought she would never see them again. She sounded as if she knew something no one else knew, but as always I was there to comfort her, giving her positive words of wisdom and letting her know she would see them again. Home deprivation was a constant struggle, it was hard to separate your love ones but it was something that had to be done in order for you to keep your sanity and yet many found it hard to do. As soon as I could finish the last words of encouragement the sirens went off again and we were told to MOPP. It was unbelievable I could not imagine this was happening all over again but it was. I couldn't put my protective gear on fast enough because I started to panic as if her words were coming to pass. They were screaming for us to get against the wall and the words bounced back and forth through the warehouse. People were everywhere. Some were putting on their gear while there were others trying to help those who were slow, it was wild I had never witness anything like this before, but it was real I didn't needed to be pinched. For the first time I can truly say I was scared! As I sat on the floor between a Major and Sergeant, who were both familiar to me, I began to tremble and hyperventilate (I couldn't breathe) in my mask. This incident had really taken me for a loop, because I had mopped many times before and had slept in my mask as well, but I had never felt like this before. I began to think irrational and the only thing I could think of was death, and how I wasn't going home.

As I began to shift my thoughts to something positive I saw my entire life flash before me. I then felt a hand patting me on my thigh as if to comfort me and a voice saying, "It's going to be all right, just take some slow breaths." I was too scare to take the advice and little did he know my whole life had just video'd before me, so I continued to hyperventilate, until I heard another voice on the opposite side saying, "It's okay, take it easy, everything is going to be all right." My thoughts were too scattered at that time to think of anything they were saying, but I had to focus my thoughts on something else and what greater thought to think of was the Lord; although, I could hear the voices of so many echoing throughout the warehouse. I started to talk to myself encouraging myself to not worry and asked the Lord to help me. I immediately heard the voice of GOD SAY, **"OH YE**

OF LITTLE FAITH, HAVE I EVER FORSAKEN YOU," and then I said, "No you haven't, but what do you want me to do here?" And then the voice answered in a soft voice, to **SAVE SOULS**. I must have passed out after this because when I awoke a new morning had already arisen and the entire night had passed away. I had slept the remainder of the night with full gear on as I laid against the wall. I don't remember when I went sleep, but one thing I am sure of, it was God who had put his comforting arms around me and had taken away the fear. Not only was this a new day, it was also a new beginning for me. I had been given a mission. I was expected to deliver what was asked of me and thereby began to live life in a different way. I thought of all kinds of ideas on how this was going to happen, but I really didn't have to, the Lord would allow this to happen by using me as the vessel. I also knew the Chaplain and the Assistant Chaplain were within my reach and were there when my soul search for ideas were over. I chasten myself to walk, talk differently and to stop smoking. I was so excited I could not wait to write home to tell my family of the good news. Life had become so much more important now, not that it wasn't important before, but now I had something specific to do, and I knew what it was. I had now figured out why I was sent to Saudi. I began to read my Bible often, and to focus not so much on the war, and its outcome but on God. Being spiritual I knew if I took care of his business he would definitely take care of mine. I started to find myself enlightened by spiritual troops, I even found myself talking more to the Assistant Chaplain which was easy to do; one because she was a female and two because of her dedication and love for Christ. She began to show me things through the spiritual eye and gave me incentive words to pursue. I was ecstatic, and a new creature in Christ. The only thing that was against me I was not able to let go of those cigarettes. Satan knew my weakness and he tried to keep me in bondage, but I still would not let that destroy what I was given to do. It seemed like the more I prayed, the more I smoked.

The evening approached and I wanted to write home, but what I wanted more was to hear my family voices, it was only a thought that wasn't going to happen so I wrote to them and told them of the good news. I was saddened, because I wanted them to know now, but I knew the mail would take weeks before they would received it. Prior to my leaving I had requested of my husband to send me some things. I needed, a mirror, some tea, lipstick and a small lamp that I would be able to use without electricity. I was still waiting and I didn't worry that much about it since I knew the mail sucked.

Once I finished my writing and everything else I was able to do I was ready for bed. As a ritual I always listened to CNN before I went to sleep and tonight was no different. But it really was different; I wanted to sleep so I took 25 mg of Benadryl. I didn't want the antihistamine effect; I just wanted to sleep the entire night. I was neatly snug in my sleeping bag on my cot, with my earplugs firmly secured on my ears, when I suddenly heard voices of hysteria and the hands of a Captain patting me. When I did awaken, most of the troops were fully in their Mopped gears. I was dumbfounded, in a stupor; I could not bring myself to wake up. Everything was happening so fast, voices of MOPP 4 were echoing, sirens were screeching through the warehouse. It was terrible, MOPP 4 were sounding through the bullhorn continually bouncing off the walls of the warehouse. Finally, I gathered my thoughts and allowed myself to get dressed, but I needed help to snap the pants and jacket because I was still in a daze. If unfamiliar with what MOPP 4 is, (it's a protective suit, which consists of a facemask, thick protective pants and top, rubber boots and gloves). This protective gear is usually worn in the event we are attacked by chemical agents, such as nerve agents like mustard gas that can caused blisters and respiratory failure and then death if untreated. We were not sure whether our allied would resort to chemical warfare, but we were not taking any chances. We were prepared for the worst, and we were lucky to have had the extensive training for such a disaster. We were told to remain calm, like that was easy to do and stay close, but my bladder didn't see it that way at all and so I needed to excrete that excess water that accumulated during the evening. If you ever wanted a difficult task to do, try using the rest room with man made plywood toilets with full protective gear on in the dark with a beam of flashlight. It's not only cumbersome it takes a lot of energy. It was seventh heaven when they announced the all clear signal and nothing at that time would please me more, than taking this garment off and having the headphones glued to my ears again. This was only the beginning; little did we know sleep would become obsolete. It was January 17, 1991, and ground war had begun. The day would go by quickly, but the night would be a living nightmare. Saddam Hussein had started his mission and for some reasons he seemed to like the night, because that's when he would direct his soldiers to blast off his scud missiles. It was useless trying to get some sleep, it seemed every night about 1 a.m. he would start his nonsense; and mopping in full gear was beginning to be a way of life for me. This rage went on for several days sometimes 2 and 3 times a night, it had gotten so bad that I began to sleep in my protective suit without much hesitation, only because as soon as you got comfortable the sirens and voices of hysteria would come. While I listened to CNN it was said that Israel had been attacked and a child had suffocated in their protective mask. I was heartbroken and saddened by the news because this child was innocent and had nothing to do with the illness of a coward. I cannot begin to tell you the anger I felt, this kind of death was senseless and Saddam Hussein had no boundaries or compassion. This man had to be self-centered and cold and sicken by his own selfishness. I thought of the people who had lost theirs lives and it sickened me to think that death could be seconds away, but did they know that? Were they prepared for it? Had they made amends? I could not understand the viciousness of a war or the tyranny it had caused. Trying very hard to refocus my anger I began to concentrate on peace and much prayer, but one thing was imminent, this monster had to be stopped. Soon didn't come easy and the war had just begun. As I lay on my cot, thoughts of despair raced through my mind, a new day was about to come. As the next several days went by the usual things happened; fear tactics upon fear tactics. I awoke one night only to hurriedly MOPP in our protective clothing, awaiting the big boom, but nothing occurred, just waiting. They were bombing everywhere, especially in Baghdad. They liked to bomb at night because it was better to maneuvered. Israel was also constantly being attack by Hussein's army, but the President of Israel had pleaded with the United States that we don't retaliate, nothing had changed, just the usual. Another quiet night went by, no sirens going off and we were able to get some sleep, but I was awaken at 3 a.m. to discover I had an accident; my nerves had cause this to happen; thank God I didn't wet my sleeping bag; can you imagine me washing that out?

A good morning transpired. I went to work. I had a leadership class with the chief nurse and other soldiers, it was informative, and done very well. My day continued with excitement. I went to the PX store to buy some goodies. I had a great dinner (fried chicken). Camp was quiet, and that in itself was scary, because we were always waiting for the big boom, or the constant echoing of sirens screeching since it has been several days and we hadn't heard from the monster, but we enjoyed the quiet time while it last; although, we remained walking on egg shells. Maybe, I had talked too soon, it's was 10:30 a.m. and there was a big blast. An explosion was heard, alarm sirens sounded, soldiers were running for cover and trying to MOPP into their protective clothing, it was its usual craziness, but we were getting into plenty of practice. Hussein is working overtime this morning, what a way to be greeted. It seemed as though it was a never-ending thing with this monster. That horror didn't last long. As usual, once it quieted down we were able to carry on with our duties of the day.

Another day has come and nothing much was going on so a drive into town was always a go. This time I got a chance to talk to my husband and that really made me feel great. It was always good to talk to the family; they always seemed to get you through the day. After our emotional needs were met we headed to the PX to stock up on some goodies for our trip into the desert, just in case.

PATRIOT MISSILE LAUNCHER USA

Chapter 9

The Desert & The Storm

I, like so many others had survived the turmoil and frustrations of a war. This morning was not unusual than any other morning, but there were rumors we were relocating to desert terrains. At first it didn't dawn on me, that we were closer into the war zone. It was probably my way to deny the unpleasantness that had became my daily life; or maybe it was the fear of not really knowing what would lie ahead of me. Honestly, I really didn't know what to think, or feel. My thoughts of staying focus on why I was here, and my obligation as a soldier/nurse, and my new found mission to save souls, was all that mattered to me: besides staying alive to see my family. I wasn't afraid, I had trusted in my Father in Heaven, and I knew he would take care of me.

Several days had past and I found myself doing the same ole things, but this day was different, we were going into town to make some phone calls. It had been a while since I was able to speak to my family and that would really make my day, so I set off into the city of Dhahran with the rest of the anxious soldiers, who had the same idea in mind. I was very happy, I talked to my husband, my daughter, my son and my sister who boo-hooo'd most of the conversation; they too were happy to hear from me. Nothing much had changed; we were doing the same ole, same ole, waiting for the big day to depart; to what we all have known to be our safe habitat.

It's another day and as usual most of us have not received a good night's sleep. Saddam Hussein started his nonsense again. It seems as though the monster was using his strategy well. I believe his mission was to make us extremely exhausted, tired us out, confuse us, by simply bombing us late into the night. The military was not buying it, nor was my platoon going to allow this monster to win, nor were we going to allow this monster to spoil any part of our day or night. I prepared myself to go into town as fast as I could, so I could make phone calls and do a little shopping at the PX. My funds were low so I decided to get an advanced payment once I arrived into town. When we returned back to the compound, we started packing, only to be told that we would not be leaving until tomorrow. So, we found ourselves unpacking and trying to find the items we needed for the moment.

Another day had come and we have survived the scuds. We were still breathing. We were alive. It is amazing how most of us looked forward to another day, only because we looked forward to spending some time at the PX and making phone calls. We were reasoning about having our meals prepared by the Saudi's men, so we were not starving. Some of us have not been able to adjust to the spicy foods, but it damned sure beats those military MRE's. Today before we will be departing our place of refuge. It has been a rewarding experience; however, I am looking forward to the move. As with many others, I prepared myself for the journey. Because there weren't any briefings given by our Commander, I knew that there was something in the air. As fear grew on the faces of many soldiers, many had the look of relief, including myself. I was really glad our mission was about to begin. We were about to enter into a journey of terrains of the unknown. Finally, we were about to do our mission to the fullest. We were about to fight for our country and save lives. By the afternoon, we were going to leave the prison warehouse: that once kept us from danger and harm behind the steel walls, and the hysteria echoes during the scud missiles attacks, which kept us without much sleep. I walked the grounds trying to find solitary; I wanted something to hold on to from the expectation that I was not sure of. I thought about the consequences of life that could be destroyed if we were not on top of things; but most of all, I thought about the efficiency of the medical equipment and staff in a given crisis. So many thoughts were pounding back and forth in my head. I thought about the 58,000.00 Vietnam troops, who have lost their lives and the POW's (prisoners of war) and MIA's (soldiers missing in action), who were never found, and the triumphs, and despair their families suffered yesterday, and today, some knowing that their love ones will never return home and some holding onto the word 'hope' . . . I just thought for a second, what if that loved one was me? I then began to think about how my family would feel if it was me. I began to ponder my thoughts and questioned the thought; did I leave my family financially secure? Or will the reading of my will be read right, or how will they survive without me? There were so many unanswered thoughts, but only to be answered if I would die at the hands of war. After all, I had no control of my destiny; I was too many miles to walk away. I was obligated to the Army and my country and in no way was I going to be labeled a coward since I had the opportunity to go. I allowed myself to pray for peace, and a speedy return home. As I walked the dessert, the sunrays beamed on my head, as if my hat was not in its proper place. So, I decided to return to the warehouse. While I was walking back, I felt a serene of peace that clouded over me; fear and doubt were no longer there. Once present inside the warehouse, the loud voices chatter bounced back and forth against the walls while the troops packed and rearranged their belongings to prepare for our departure. To my surprise, we were given a mini briefing and were told that we will be departing at 8 p.m., but being flexible as we were, we did not leave until 10 p.m., and we had become accustomed to this.

    The sky darkened and the stars became visible almost in arms reach, as we drove the terrains in the night. I sat next to my favorite Sergeant and we chatted until sleep took hold on us both. Awaken by the bumpy roads, we were given the options to use the rest room if we needed to go, so we hurried off the buses, only to discover there were no rest rooms, just the terrains and the bodies of each other to cover, as we squatted to empty our bladders. Many felt embarrassed as they had to expose their buttocks to the bare air and not to mention the ones who could not completely squat while they felt the perverts on the bus watched and giggled at the nudity of their asses. When all were finished, we boarded the buses with quickness, only to discover we were lost. It seemed like we drove forever, some say forty hours in the desert, but it was about seventy-two hours to me, it felt like a decade until we came upon a unit who were cooking breakfast from Aunt Jemima teachings, at least it smelled that way. The bacon and eggs were on my mouth and lips and at last, I was going to eat and reminiscence as though I was home. As all of the commanders discussed directions, others and I stood in lines to get a decent meal, including real coffee and tea. To some and myself, this venture was considered seventh heaven and to others, this was not a priority. I called it a mere blessing. After a good tasting meal, we boarded the buses to continue to our destination; at least most of us were pretty well full and happy. My girlfriend and I chatted as we road the bumpy terrain together. Our conversation was not amounting to anything, but we mumbled on to pass the time away, we conversed about past experiences and our love ones left at home. Our main conversations were geared to what our expectations were and how we were going to handle the war situation when it came. As we drove passed many unknown places, a sunbeam penetrated against the windows and the heat pierced our faces as if we were lying on a sunny beach insisting on a tan. The desert was a strange place. "How could any one live in such an environment that seemed so empty and isolated," I thought, as we passed through terrain; we passed several houses that looked like huts, unkempt camels, and sheep staggered everywhere. Sheep and camel were of no isolation as like chicken and bacon are our number one meat; sheep and camels are theirs. I did notice that the females and children were the only ones attending to the sheep. The women were of strange existence. They wore black attire that covered their whole body and the only expose parts were their eyes and part of their hands and their nails were painted with Henna. I later learned the ones who dress in that entirety were the married ones. The houses were built far apart. They looked shabby, worn and covered with sand dust, brick partitions encased the house to keep the sand away, but it really didn't do any good. I wonder if these people were neighbors. As we journeyed across the desert, it seemed as though everything disappeared and we were the only ones left on the universe. We finally arrived to our location. We were deep in the desert and it was very dark and the only thing we saw to remind us of greenery was our camouflage battle dress uniform that we wore, which was almost impossible to see because of the sand dust. The advanced party had left earlier to prepare our stay and arrival. They left early so they could set up our tents before we arrive. It was very unorganized. Hunger and sleep desperately haunted me, along with so many others. Finally, our tent location was established and we quickly settled in. The bathrooms were located one quarter of a mile from our tents, and of course, it did not take long to get acquainted. Most of the officers were gathered in the same tents, which was not unusual, since that was the military protocol. Not that we were better than the enlisted, but we were officers in charge and held to a higher standard. Some of the enlisted resented the fact that we were getting special treatment or to the fact, we were officers. I thought this kind of thinking was foolish, who cared anyway, besides we were at war, guns and bullets had no ranks on them. The morning started with MREs, canteen of water, and kerosene heaters to tidy our bodies. It was not a hard task, but uncomfortable trying to wash in private areas with so many present, but it had to be done and it was something you quickly became used to. After our hurry, semi-wash, a cigarette and a hot cup of tea was in order. The morning was bright, without the smell of dew I was comfortable to know at last we were at our destination. Echoes of good mornings cheered back and forth as people passed along each other to their respected places and duties. It was a good morning and I thanked God for allowing us to reach safely, sleep well and arise again. As the morning subsided into noon, I could not help wonder what my children were doing at this time, since their time zones were different, for us it was morning, but for the United States, it was night. If I only could call them to let them know that I was okay and still alive and would be home soon, that would really blossom my day. Although I tried desperately not to focus much on home and my family, there were moments when I just wanted and needed my husband to hold me and reassure me that everything was going to be all right. It seemed as though time was drifting slowly by, and the days seemed so much longer, as if another morning would never approach. But the next morning did come. The talk was always happening, rumors were always flying. Today was no special morning, same ole, same ole, although we did discover that another unit was east of us and most of all visible, which took away many apprehensions and made it easy to know that we were not the only ones in the desert. As the day progressed, we learned that a few more units surrounded us. Rumors had surfaced that our commander was making arrangements for us to use the showers. Meetings were held as usual and faces grew flush as days continued. Formation was held to discuss the possibility that we were going to change to a MASH unit. Meaning only 240 troops were able to go as a MASH and the rest who were not chosen were going to be alternating to other units, since we were over strength. Of course this new added burden was stressful to worry about, and left most of us looking trouble, not knowing if we were going to be split up or not. This really had me down, because the last thing I wanted was to be separate from my unit. I tried hard not to think about it, but that seemed to be the concerns and conversations of many troops. Trying to avoid the new added burden was impossible. I thought of how ludicrous it would be if they did this, after all I could have stayed in the United States with my wounded feet if I really did not want to be here. It was awful, but what else could be more awful than wanting a cold shower about now and not being able to have one. I laid on my cot thinking about "the what ifs," that I decided to read to alter my thoughts on something else, but the thoughts of being separated and having to learn new troops kept pulling on me. A tap on the tent door and a voice calling for Loretta usually meant a cigarette, and as always I went for it. The night could not have come at a better time, since the night always seemed to calm me. A still in the night. A time to rejuvenate and entertain thoughts of the daily events that somehow faded but the memory was always there. This time allotted me to pray to my savior. It always seemed so proper to pray to my savior at night. I had this feeling that He heard you better since it seemed to be much quieter, I thought. It seemed as thought He could concentrate on me more, at least that is how I pictured it. My prayers were always straight to the point, I always started with forgiveness, because I knew somewhere during the day, I probably sinned, but not intentionally of it. "Oh God, forgive me of my sins in the name of Jesus. Lord, I thank you for waking me up and for protecting me another day. I would ask that He blessed my family and keep them in his perfect will, in the name of Jesus." I prayed that the Lord bless my Commander and my leaders in charge of this mission; let their decisions be decisive and most of all pleasing to the Lord. "Don't allow me to be separated from my troops, I prayed, in the name of Jesus, but Lord, allow the war to end quickly, and don't forget to bless those men, women, and children, who are innocent in the name of Jesus, and please bless the troops and their families." The prayer was no different. I always seem to pray basically for the same thing, but I felt so much at peace at night once I did. Morning was here again and this morning, a decision had to be made. Butterflies raced through my stomach as I prepared for the day. There was nothing much to do around the desert, but chat a lot, and walk a little, which seemed to allow the day to pass quicker. I visited friends in other tents and chatted with others. While I was chatting with friends, a briefing was called immediately. We gathered around the chief in command and we were told that a decision had been made. We were also told not to take it personally, if your name was not called. He also informed us that the decision was based on the needs of the MASH unit. As I waited in anticipation to hear my name, it was never called. Once the meeting adjourned, I walked silently back to my tent, trying hard to hold back the tears, but I could feel them streaming down my face. I did not know what to think. I felt cold and numb and as stages of grieving progressed, I felt a sense of denial surfacing, this could not be happening to me, but it was. As the officers entered the tent, they too were upset and some of them were crying, while some of them tried to be strong for the rest of us. It was a sad day today and the only thing that could rectify it; it was that the day was not really happening. Although we tried to console each other sadness, it was almost impossible. We were being separated and the war would need us in different units, but not all of us together. As my chief nurse entered the tent, I asked her if I could speak with her. My questions to her were, "If you all knew that we were over strength as nurses, then why didn't this split take place in the United States?" Why wait until we are a thousand miles away to separate us. I explained my importance, why I should have been chosen, because of my MOS and my qualification as a nurse, and my specialty in med-surgery (medical surgical nurse, a nurse that specialized and have the knowledge in all physically systems of the body). I also expressed my concern of the nurses being chosen that has not worked daily or who were currently in opposed to those who do work daily in their MOS and were not chosen. She allowed me to express my concerns and tried to comfort me in saying, they tried to make the best decision, but little did I know then, that the decision made was the best decision ever made for me and others that were not separated. God always has a way of working things out, doesn't He? I guess it did matter since I wasn't going to be with her, you see she was my idol, I learned a lot from her and to be separated from her was like being separated from an angel. She was a walking knowledge, full of wisdom and experiences most of all, she carried herself with so much confidence, that when she entered a room, her presence made a statement; everyone stopped whatever they were doing and literally came to attention, in a sense of speaking. She was powerful, another Mr. Colin Powell. She was my role model. Poised and so positive. She talked with a direct articulate speech and her voice was electrifying with every word perfectly pronounced, and if I could be anybody in the world besides Mary, Jesus' mother, I would be honor to be her. And now, I was not going to have the opportunity to be with my hero; I was going to be sent off with people I didn't know, and who didn't know me. The hope I had, I had lost because I felt betrayed, but only temporary. I did not care at that moment. I was angry, like the others that were going to be sent somewhere else. There were a few officers who decided to stay up to chat, and boil hot water for coffee and tea, so I decided to join them also. The chief nurse placed her canteen of water on the kerosene heater, only to come back with tissue floating inside of it. Until today, I cannot remember how it happened. But I do know she gave a speech of rude awareness and she was very upset; the tissue was in her cup, but no one had no idea how it got in there and we were not at fault. I honestly think it was an accident, I could not imagine any officer doing something so silly to a lady regarded to high standards. When she left, some found it funny and giggled about it, of course, behind her back. There were also some friction between the supply and the mess officer, as who was going and why they were not chosen. The bickering continued until the supply officer was reassigned to another position and was going to be reunited with the unknown. But if ranks have its privileges, the Major sure beats the hell out of Captain every time. As for me, I was only a butterbar respecting the Lieutenant, so I definitely did not have much to say. I finally retired, settled in my cot, zipped from head to toe in my sleeping bag as usual and said my daily prayers as always.

Chapter 10

We're Ready

Allies

1991 Saudi Arabia Tanker

Today most of the troops knew where they were going, except a handful of us. Some were preparing to leave as soon as they got the go ahead when they were ordered to. Although many of us wanted to know what was going on, as usual nothing much was said. Once again, we were in the dark. The majority of them would be leaving tomorrow, so they were preparing as well. Breakfast, lunch, and dinner consists of MRE's, or whatever you had to eat, but it was too hot and too frustrating to eat, but I managed to force myself to nibble on crackers and peanut butter since that became my delicacy. One of the Captains was also departing, so she asked my assistance in washing her hair. It was hilarious trying to wash and rinse her hair in a small basin; although it was different we had a fun time doing it. After all, we needed that sense of humor, since we were going to be separated sooner than we wanted to, and who knew if humor would ever surface again, or if we would see each other again. I would miss her because she was witty and funny. She always had something to say; she was enlightened, even though sometimes, it was not at all funny. It was really happening, she was leaving me too. Although she hugged and gave me words of peace, I could not help but think she too would also be a lost. My closest officers were leaving and it was hard to say goodbye. As I walked around the compound, I visited motor pool, only to find them very busy and getting ready for their departure, that I knew I didn't want to take place, but it was going to happen whether I wanted it or not. After all, it was not me who was in charge, nor did I make those decisions. I was there to fulfill our mission and that was to be an army nurse and to take care of the casualties. As they approached the five-tons the next day, those who were left behind gathered together to say their goodbyes. Many hugs and well wishes were given, it was not easy. I began to cry again, like so many others. When everyone was aboard the five-ton, we stood there, chatted comforting words towards each other while the engine started and we drove off into the desert. The day seemed dreary, almost as if we were the forgotten rebels, but they did leave us a few benches behind, but that too would soon be forgotten; they were to return and take the remaining. I am not sure how it came about, but we were also told that we had to relocate. We were informed that another unit was coming to greet us and they were going to make accommodation available to us. They did not come right away, but our unit did return to take the various items they had left behind. They left us with no lights, some bottled water, probably a case, if accurate, no benches to sit on, no showers, and if remembering correctly, two Manmade bathrooms, not to mention very few MREs. Luckily, we had bathroom privileges with the 340Th MASH and took full advantage of that unit. We were able to make arrangements for meals with the 31st CASH, who stayed about a half a mile or more from us, who took us under their wings, fed us and gave us light and kerosene. Our unit just left us, in a sense, bone dry, but as in any war, you will survive according to the military, and yet we are all one. A captain visited our tents, made herself acquainted and invited us to watch a movie in their recreation tent, and we took her up on that offer. The 31st CASH was our refuge in a sense; they were there for us. We were able to enjoy hot meals and most of all nice showers. The only downfall, we were given a time to shower and had to wait until they showered. As the night fell, we surrounded ourselves together in the tent. I was with my lieutenant friend, who was Caucasian and complained about everything, but we managed to get along just fine. I think she was just over zealous or just anxious. There were other officers in the tent who bunked with us, but we were outnumbered by the enlisted. Most of the tents were filled with enlisted troops, the ones that were left, but we got along just fine. We were all learning to adjust, learning the true meaning of survival, until we got orders of where we would be relocating. Most of the time, if we were not reading, playing cards, some of us chatted to pass along the time. Although we had much time on our hands, we did look at it as that; we were more concerned about what the next happening would be. Most of the troops were angry with our unit for leaving us like they did, but we somehow managed to focus our negative energies into positive energies, such as meeting new soldiers, finding solitude in ourselves, and simply taking one day at a time. That is exactly what I did, I decided to go over to the 31st CASH and enjoy my first shower in weeks. It was beautiful to allow the running water to drip on my head and to lather my entire body from head to toe and most of all to have privacy. I know you can not imagine the feeling I had, but if you ever were a winner or could imagine yourself winning a lottery, then you can imagine the euphoric I had. After my shower, I decided to take the captain's invitation to watch movies in the recreation tent. It was a social event. Men and women were enjoying every minute of it, laughing and indeed having a good time. I thought that this is exactly what I needed, a time to relax. After all I was clean and in a sense in seventh heaven. The only downfall, the movie only lasted less than two hours and it was to return over the hump to the real world, (I at that time thought only existed, I was not aware of the unit until then). My lieutenant roommate complained as usual how home sick she was, and how much she hated it, but I was missing home, missing mostly my husband, my children, and my dog very much, but what could I do about it now, absolutely nothing, but to write home as often as I could. I was informed the next day, we would have formation with the 31st CASH. I felt good, that finally something was happening and I was no longer in the dark, at least that was the step in a positive direction, whatever it was worth. Although it did not matter at that time, at least I was part of a team and they were playing. Later on that night, we heard trucks and loud noises pull into our compound, to our surprise, it was another unit.

Later we learned, this was the unit from Washington, D.C. that was unable to perform their mission. Our unit became a MASH and went forward. Being curious, we greeted them and tried to assist them in getting situated. Formation was early as usual, six a.m. in full uniform with protective equipment, which was not too hard to do, since that seemed to be the daily attire these days. We were given the password to allow us passage from one compound to another, and we were there bright and early standing at ease, waiting for the commander to make his appearance. We got acquainted and to my surprise, I was the squad leader. During the first formation of the day, I met a friend, who I still stay in touch with, as of today. She was a Captain, and because she was short in statue, and I ate beanie and weenies, secretly we decided to name ourselves "Beanie and Weenie" and of course, I was Beanie. She was from Washington, D.C., and we hit it off well, as if we knew each other for years. We became buddies; we did almost everything together. We had a lot of things in common, a family at home, and children. Although, she looked very stern, she was very much afraid, she too like myself had no expectation of the unknown. I don't think I was afraid like she was because of my spiritual background and beliefs, but there were times when I thought I was never ever going to see home again and I prayed not to return home in a body bag. We became partners, inseparable. Every time you saw me, you saw her. We talked a lot together, ate meals together, and smoked together. We became a team, Beanie and Weenie; everywhere we went they knew us. Not to say we were popular or anything of that sort, just good buddies. Early formation was usually called and Weenie was always half sleep or complaining of her aching feet. That was covered with bunions and she was given permission to wear sneakers until her feet were better. At first, she would talk about everything, except her family, I detected that she was having problems at home, but she was not open about those issues. Her main purpose was to get out of Saudi Arabia and return home and she did not care how it would happen or what it was going to take, as long as it happened. Formation was different this morning; we had to do task skills, by running around the compound with our protective suits and masks on in full gear. To complete the task, we had to drink out of our canteen bottles with our protective masks on. This task was not at all that difficult for those and myself since we received this readiness training in Fort Stewart prior to coming here. It was tiresome, many soldiers were out of shape and some stopped running and a few of them passed out. This task seemed like it lasted for many hours but it only lasted a few minutes, which definitely was enough time for me. But running in those protective suits with 110 degree weather in sand is indeed a difficult task. After our daily exercise, word had it that we were leaving the compound and moving forward, closer to the Kuwait border to set up our hospital. I was excited, but the Captain and some of the Lieutenants, only thoughts were to go home. As for me, I knew that the expectation of the unknown was about to unravel and we had a destination and a full mission ahead. I believed in the military. I knew we had ourselves together, and we were going to win, no matter what happened, after all we had lost too many lives senselessly before in the Vietnam war, and our leaders were not going to repeat that ever again. So, I was ready to do my mission, to focus on my position as an army nurse. I did not allow my friends to discourage me; I always tried to stay focused on why I was here. The evening was pretty quiet, except for the usual noises of the trucks, cars, planes, and girl talk, which continued just about every evening. After our wash off in the tents, we decided to make hot cocoa, which became a ritual every evening, we really looked forward to it. The evenings were always filled with unity in our tent, some would say it seemed like we were one big happy family and we were. Our gatherings were always focused on the happenings of the day, events, and what was to become of the outcome. After chatting for several hours, we were exhausted and drifting one by one to sleep.

Chapter 11

Making A Connection

I awakened as usual to my daily activities of the day, breakfast, formation, and daily briefings of the day. After formation, we were given the opportunity to go into town to make phone calls. I could not believe it, but I made every effort to be in line. As we boarded the fiveton with full gear on, including our protective mask, I was finally going to hear the voices of my family. I was indeed overwhelmed by the idea and could not help the feelings of the palpitations that went along with joy. As we drove through the sandy terrain, sand blew in our faces, as if to discourage us from completing our journey; but that certainly was not going to happen, after all, we were too excited to turn back, so we endured the sandy winds as it blew in the air. Once we reached our destination, there was a huge crowd of troops gathered in line, and little did I know that it was for the use of the phones. We jumped off the five-tons to be a part of the patience troops, who stood anxiously as they waited their turn. Some chatted with each other; some puffed on cigarettes, while others stood blankly. The buses waited several hours while we used the phones. We were only allotted ten to fifteen minutes to speak with our love ones and then to hike that long ride almost two and half hours back. The long ride wasn't all that bad, just having the opportunity to speak to a love one was well appreciated, and well worth it, and well deserving, but it was always sad to hang up; at least for me, because I wanted to stay focus on my mission. As I watched the faces of my buddies, I could see darkness of uncertainty, the not knowing if this call was going to be our last one, but their faces always seemed to sparkle until they were given the one-minute signal, which meant we had to end our conversations. When we arrived back to the compound, lunch had already been served and supper chow was about to happen, so we gathered in a line to feast on whatever was available. I am not saying that the food wasn't good, but most of the time it was: lukewarm canned ravioli, beef stroganoff, jam, and peanut butter, and if reward was in order, we could have hot potatoes or mash potato, but on the whole, the food was so much better than what I was use to.

After a shower, there was not a whole lot to do, sometimes we would walk around the compound, and as to pretend we were doing a whole lot. My buddy and I had developed a good friendship and we would talk extensively about home. Sometimes I would have to cut her short in the middle of the conversation, because she would get carried away. She had an obsession of home, as though she knew if she stayed, she would not return, and that sometimes made me think, "What if?" As I lay in my cot, I was amazed by the trembling vibrations of the ground, I thought we were being bombed within several feet away, but it was the ricochet affect of the bombs many miles away. It was hard to sleep at night, so I placed my earphones to listen to CNN, only to learn that bombing was taking place and lives were being lost. It was an eerie feeling. I knew we were moving closer tomorrow to the Kuwaiti border (1 kilometer) to construct our hospital, to care for the casualties that were stricken by injuries.

Chapter 12

Getting Closer

The plan of the day was announced we were going closer to the Kuwait border. We gathered into groups to tear down the tents and clean outside the compound, as if no one ever rested there. It was hard work and it seemed as though it would never end. We huddled in groups to the five-tons without belongings to head for our new site somewhere in the midst of the desert. No one actually knew our true destination and if they did it was of higher authority and if they did tell us, we was always given the story of ten-fifteen kilometers away from the Kuwait borders, except it didn't tell us much. As we drove through the terrains, we stopped several times to use the restrooms and to have a bite to eat and drink. To some, smoking of cigarettes was all that was needed. My buddy and I stayed close together as we rode into the night, listening to yacky yak and concern voices; and the running engine as we convoyed through the desert. So many thoughts were racing through my head, and I can not remember how I actually felt until that morning. I felt desolated and missing, my previous home, because I had gotten so use to where I was before. I knew the quicker we got to where we were going, the faster our mission would be completed. We finally arrived to our site, sometime during the night and boy! Was it dark, and the earth seemed so still. The advanced party had reached before us to set up tents, which some were initiated and we took advantage of the establishment and embedded ourselves when we could find rest. So many bickered about our new accommodation, but it had gotten them, absolutely no where. Morning came too fast, as it always did, to make us feel as if we did not sleep at all. The new tents were constructed with the help of military personnel, including the additional officers. One thing about the 31st CASH, their officers had no problems assisting, or for that matter initiating a task. I guess it was not unusual since they were active duty. Don't misunderstand, I am not saying reservist does not perform their mission, but some of them have the tendency of being gunho or weekend warriors, especially the ones in authority. Most of the time, the OIC (officer in charge) officers higher ranking enlisted, and the NOIC (noncommissioned officers), get their kicks being totally in charge for two days. I sometimes think some of them prepare themselves just for the weekend drill on the weekend, and it wouldn't surprise me, if they stood in front of the mirror and practiced. The Colonel was Dawn Richards, so when she walked in a room full of loud chatter, a silence would erupt almost immediately, if they looked up and saw it was Colonel Richards. She was something special; she had "air" about herself, but somehow always intimidated most people, and was not very well appreciated by many soldiers. At first, I was also afraid of her myself but I later understood her agenda. She had such an articulation speech and charismatic about her, you would agree with almost anything she said, even though you disagreed, just because of who she was and you didn't want her to explain anything else in detail. But she had that way about her, but on the other hand, I admired this lady to the point, I often wished I could be just like her. I guess she had an honest approach. If you wanted to know anything about the military, she was definitely the one to ask.

Washing in a basin, heating water by a kerosene heater was great, but having a real shower was needed. When I went to take a shower, I heard noises of passion. It was hard for me to see who they were since it was dark inside, so I just took my shower as if no one was there and of course when I finished, they too had stopped. That type of behavior was not unusual, as a matter of fact; it was becoming increasingly the thing to do. I could never imagine being unfaithful to my husband, even though he had been unfaithful to me. I believed in commitment, but for some reason, these people had their vows mixed up. I can only say, that I was doing the right thing, I just prayed that my husband was feeling the same way too. On the other hand, I was many miles away and that gave him plenty of room if he wanted to. Actually, I never thought much about sex, I swear they were putting something only in my food since I didn't have an increased libido and remained faithful with just a handful of others. Probably because I was so involved in Christ's word, that I didn't have time to think about sex. The day eventually turned out well, the hospital was about to be constructed and soon we would be in operation, and we would be expected for sure to carry on with our mission.

Chapter 13

Depmeds

The plan was to set up the hospital. My buddy was complaining about her feet that evening and decided to go to sick call in the morning. There was another officer who had dropped a box on her feet and was unable to walk, later she learned her feet were actually swollen and broken, but she continue to attend formation with those boots on, but it was not knowing after, that she had permission to wear sneakers. My buddy went to sick call, along with so many others. She did get quarters (no duties) but she did not get the news she wanted to hear, to return to Conus (United States), but she was allowed to wear her sneakers. Sick call was crowded. Some of those troops were not sick; some of them wanted to go home. I knew my friend had bunions, but I am not sure she had them before she came, but she did have blisters. She creeped around with a limp for a few days, and complain continuously about going home. I tried to support her emotions, but nothing I said helped, she wanted out, like so many others. Her mind was only preoccupied on her daughter and her boyfriend, but she did not say a word as to what was happening. She received quarters for a day or two, and I catered to her every need and I believe she was appreciative. But when her quarters were up, she continued to limp around, while her facial expression drooped with sadness and her expressions, said "do not ask me to work." Preparation of the hospital was in order. Most of the troops were eager to see the hospital completed. A day of work began normally soon after breakfast. We were divided into groups and were given instructions on how the hospital would be constructed. There were several groups composed of ten to twenty enlisted and officer personnel who were ready to work. Depmeds was familiar training to me, and most of the reservists. The active duty troops were not efficient with Depmeds as we were. Depmeds were knowledgeable to the reserve component, only because we constantly trained with it during our annual training (two weeks out of a year). Depmeds is another word used for hospital (it is a field hospital), if you can remember the TV sitcom Mash you can pretty much get the idea which consists of everything just like you would find in a regular hospital. The unit was to construct a 600 bed capacity hospital, emergency room, six ICW (immediate care wards), ICU (intensive care unit), operating rooms, and not to mention, the blood bank, lab, sick call, pharmacy, x-ray, and everything else you would find in a hospital. We were informed that this construction was to be completed within one week, and during that time, another unit would come to assist with the construction of another ICW. Our day began early in the morning as usual, unloading equipment, and constructing our hospital. The sun would be so intense, that at times it was almost impossible to continue working, and many breaks became needed, along with the drinking of much water. Although I hated to drink water, it had become my friend. We would start early in the morning with our full uniform on and in about one hour or two, our jacket shirts would come off, and our pants had to be rolled up. Beads of perspiration dripped down our faces as we would diligently work in small groups, the work was easy and fun, but it was still consider hard work. It was hard for me to notice my new complexion in my little compact mirror, but I did notice that my skin was darkening, and burning more often. I had gotten sunburn, if one doesn't believe dark skinned people get sunburn they lie because I am a living witness of it. The sun seemed like it overpowered you and sometimes it appeared to be so close you felt you could touch it. The only thing that was beautiful about the sun was when it set, it was so beautiful; rainbow colored was almost mystical as it disappeared into the sky as if it didn't exist. On our third day, the construction was looking more like a hospital as we stopped for lunch. My buddy and I would chat as we stood in the long line for chow, only to be served cold can ravioli, or beef stroganoff, something the cooks loved to feed us, or peanut butter and jelly sandwiches. Although they tried to keep the can goods warm in these huge metal pots, but for some odd reason, they always seemed to taste like aluminum, and the temperature felt as if they within minutes just drop them in. Sometimes it didn't matter because sometimes I wasn't hungry, but I tried to make the best of it. Then there were the days when I settled for that good old-fashioned peanut butter and jelly sandwich, until I discovered molded bread, and dead little flying insects in the jelly. That was the end of good old fashion sandwiches, so then it became plain peanut butter and MRE's crackers, and my eyes became more observant. Sometimes it was fight to eat, the flies would attack your food and not leave, so it became a task, swatting and waving your hands to remove them. The flies were strange, they would get on your food and did not give a damn what you did until they had their quota of it, and then only would they fly away. I only thought during those moments that I wish I could fly away too. My buddy and myself would some times skip lunch, because we got tired of the same ole, same ole, and sometimes the cigarette was so much better. We would chatter about the hard work and could not wait until it was over, at least for me; it was the hospital for her; it was the waiting for the war to be over for me. The completions inside the tents were done. Now it was time to place the floors down, which was not hard work, except for our knees, that got a hell of beating on crawling back and forth on them. Once that was done, we started to receive supplies from the mil vans to stock our hospital wards.

We were ready and we put our section up by inventory our equipment. All teams, along with others, worked long hours so we could finish at full capacity. Although it was extremely hot, we worked until we were told to quit. I have never had the opportunity to assist in reconstructing a hospital, especially a 600-bed one, and I had enjoyed every minute of it. There were times when it seem as though we would never finished, since there was so much equipment, we had to leave some on the mil vans and placed what we though we might need in storage. Lifting, arranging, adjusting, and rearranging so much equipment, it seemed almost impossible to complete. But with the help of motivated voices on our team and the direction of our ward master, we did it and had plenty of time to venture our heads with new ideas. After the completion of the ICWs, various teams investigated each other units, actually to see whose ward looked the best. I must admit, between our ward and the fifth ICW, we looked pretty organized, and resemble a civilian hospital ward. I am not saying that the other wards didn't look like a hospital but they looked more cluttered. We complimented each other anyhow for a job well done in such a little time. We were officially finished with the hospital, with the exception of installing the main pipelines for our water. I was truly amazed the hospital looked close to a real civilian one. We had an emergency room that was fully equipped, a blood bank, a lab, an ICU, an operating room that looked willing and ready to operate. After a quick bite to eat, Weenie and myself did our PM care, had some small talk, and some laughter. My routine ritual was the same, Walkman, CNN, a prayer, and sleep. I could not help of wondering, what lie ahead the next few days, since the hospital would be operable. I had seen so many movies and heard so many horror stories of Vietnam that I could almost visualize the stampedes of wounded soldiers, torn and bleeding, running to the combat medic or through the jungle with the expression of helplessness on their faces as they asked for help. But I was only daydreaming and this was not going to happen, and I was not ready in that way for horror stories. It was late, and I was indeed tired; and tiredness breathes idle thinking sometimes. However, I could not help thinking the worst was about to happen.

After a long day of hard work, we would go back to our tents. Earlier when we arrived at the compound, we assigned additional duties, and of course ours was the sanitation team. Our responsibilities were as follows: empty and clean all the latrines, restock the restrooms with toilet tissues, and burn all the waste. The job may have been demeaning but somebody had to do it. The stench would be so overwhelming that sometimes I thought I was going to regurgitate, but I allowed myself to stay calm and focus on the thought that it would one day be over. We would dig foxholes, throw the waste into them, along with gasoline, and initiate fires to eliminate the waste products. The female restrooms were always the worst their bins would be full to its capacity with whatever else they wanted to dispose of. So between finalizing the hospital and our additional duties, we were physically worn out by the evening. Once our task was completed, most of the troops, if not all, got situated in our home away from home. To me this was home, and I had to accept that and it was not hard getting us to.

The weather was real crazy here. In the morning, it would be like two degrees below zero and by 10a.m, it would be 120 degrees, and at night it would be back to two degrees below zero. The weather was unbelievable that I actually slept in two sweat suits, socks on, four blankets, and my sleeping bag zipped from head to toe. Sometimes it didn't matter what I had on; it always seemed like the cold weather just went right through you. After a MRE's dinner, a quick wash off and rest, I listened to CNN as I usually did, but nothing spectacular was happening, except for the usual bombing that was a common event about now. After all, what was Saddam Hussein going to do next? All I knew we had to beat him at his own game. The breaking of a new day had emerged and formation was in its usual time (early), but I was used to getting up at 4 a.m. so I could brush my teeth, and take my morning stroll, and visit the latrine before it got busy

Chapter 14

Ground War

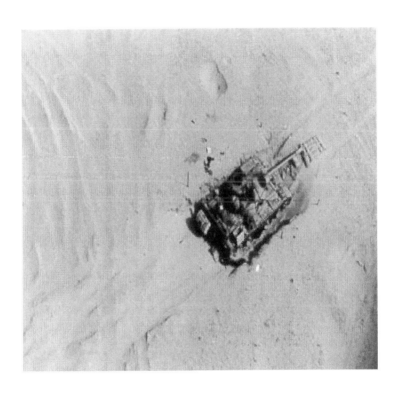

The hospital was ready and yes, we were too. We did not have formation that morning. Nothing unusual happened with most of the formation, they were becoming more redundant anyway. However today, we were assigned shifts and of course they were seven days a week with a possible one day off.

My shift was 7 p.m. to 7 a.m., which wasn't too bad. It gave me more time to sleep in and wash my clothing during the day, no other than by hand of course. The only sad thing it allowed Weenie and myself to be separated as we passed each other, she worked the 7 a.m. to 7 p.m. shift. The first day was exciting; I was the OIC nurse (officer in charge) along with another officer. The other officer was from Germany and she was someone to like and work together with. That evening was spent rearranging equipment, familiarizing our staff with the hospital equipment and paperwork. Lo and behold, we would get our first casualty, a young black soldier who said he accidentally sat on a bandanna while getting into his tanker, and who had punctured a fairly large wound to his buttock. At first it seemed serious, potential damage to his nerves, but he was lucky the nerves were intact, dressing changes with sterile techniques became our routine; but most of us wondered if he didn't inflict the wound himself, so he could escape the war. You see he operated a tanker that was very close to the Kuwait border, and he would have been right up on the front line, which probably echoed danger to his ears. That was only an after thought, after all I tried very hard to picture the accident myself and to this day I'm still unable to figure it out. Let's face it; he was not the only one, who didn't want to become a dead hero. He was young, barely 23 years old, opposition was around him, and he panicked.

M60 Tanker

There were many of them like him, babies, no understanding of a real war, other than what they had seen in movies and on television, some of them had never left the states before. We often chatted to each other; after all, he was our first casualty. He received so much attention, that he became spoiled; it was almost impossible to care for him since everyone wanted a chance. Our first few days together were strictly patient to nurse, but after caring and talking to him for a few days, he seemed like an honest guy. The other soldiers tried very hard to pry information from him to see if he knew exactly when ground war was going to start, but he didn't tell us anything for certain. If he did know, he was not letting us in on the secret. ICU was pretty busy themselves, they too had received their first patient, and there were some more following a few days later. They were patients now scattered throughout the wards. After leaving work that morning, and appreciating my usual wash off, an officer ran into the tent yelling "mash casualty, mash casualty, mash casualty." It would have been welcome if I didn't work last night; I probably would have welcomed it better. For once rumor held true that it was going to happen, we just didn't know when. But there were also other rumors that did not happen. I should have not been too anxious. If unfamiliar with mash casualty, it is a (training exercise medical task). It was definitely chaotic. People were everywhere. Gurneys were dropped off almost constantly, as soon as one gurney was unloaded; more gurneys were dropped off at the emergency room exit door. Choppers were bringing them in as fast as we got one off the gurney. But in reality this scenario was not real, but it could as well become reality if disaster happens, so this kind of exercise was an essential task and well need it. The nurses functioned in the same role they would in the civilian world. They would take patient's vital signs (blood pressure, pulse, temperature, and respiration), monitor the patient's condition, dress their wounds if they need it, assess for any type of abnormal conditions and if problems arose they would notify the medical doctor. The nurses are the eyes for the doctors. They are there to aid in the stability of the patient, as well as administer medications and give emotional support. Sparing a life is too valuable, and no one wanted their love ones to return to the states in a body bag. As army nurses these were our functions and it was no different then in the civilian world. After having the okay to leave, I returned to my tent only to snuggle myself between my blankets and sleeping bag. I did not have much sleep that evening, because I had to be to work at 7 p.m. Normally at that time, Weenie was on her way in as I was leaving, so most of the times I didn't get a chance to talk to her as much as I would have liked to. It felt awfully strange to have a buddy, who slept right next to you, but you often missed each other because of our working schedules. When we did see each other, we often hugged, chatted about current events, home, and she would always speak of the possibilities of being sent home. She was concerned about her daughter who was left with her boyfriend, but she never mentioned that she was a grandmother. She always looked trouble. She wasn't the same person, something was happening back home, and she felt to keep it to herself. I wanted to reach out to her, and reassure her everything would be fine, but sometimes it is hard to do when the other person is so many miles away. I wasn't tired for some reason, I should have been, but I guess my body was getting used to the long twelve hours.

Sergeant Block was talkative as usual, dragging his big feet across the man made rubber tile that screeched from being wet the day before. Our conversations always lend itself to question when was ground war going to start, and as usual he would estimate a day, never being exact. The evening was like any other evening. Every shift was responsible for checking their equipment, restocking supplies, and visiting the ICU's. Sergeant Block and I would often go inside the open mil van (storage room) to chat and a restricted area to smoke cigarettes when time permitted. He would try to be flirtatious and tease me, saying I was too faithful to my husband. It wasn't a joke, I was faithful. I didn't feel the need to stray.

You see I loved my husband, and my mission and marriage was far too great to risk it all. Besides, I loved Christ and his Father, and I was already being disobedient by smoking, but I had an addiction, and it was very hard to shake. However, my love for Christ did not stop me from ministering his word, and telling the soldiers the good news of who he was and what he had done for my family and me. Yet, Sergeant Block wasn't ready to give his soul, but I still continued to minister to him.

It was all too true; the ground war was in progress January 17, 1991. It was really happening. Others and I had waited so long for this day, that we were not sure if we were dreaming, or was this for real. We knew it was real, because casualties started to fill the hospital emergency room. As I was in my ward, Captain Smalls came over from the emergency room and asked for my assistance. I would hurry to the emergency room entrance only to receive second war victims as the medics transported them off the gurney. I could see blood running everywhere. As they were rushed in they were taken care of immediately. I assessed their airway, initiated IV's and of course gloving was careless, but who would concern themselves with anything else, other than airway replacing fluids, having an IV site and always to control the bleeding. The Chaplain was on hand to say a prayer while another call was radioed in to let us know that another set of casualties were on there way. Before we could maintain stability in the emergency room, the medics had already arrived. This time, it was three instead of two American soldiers. One of them had an eye bandaged from an explosion that took place in the desert. Faith had already taken its toll, he was blind in both eyes, but was not aware of his condition (blindness) yet. After the chaotic mess, things seemed to seem to settle down and we were in control again, if only for a moment. I went back to my ward, only to receive two of those casualties, the rest were sent to the operating room and other wards. The blind soldier also had scrapnel wounds to his leg, and the other had a broken leg. I could not help thinking of the sadness that their families will feel when they return. I could only thank God for allowing only his blindness and injuries, but his mercy to spare his life was much greater, I thought. But then I thought, what good is life when one cannot see, especially when they was use to sight and came there whole. It was not left up to me to judge, but I did feel sympathy of yet another fate I could not control. My only question was: how much more suffering were we allowed to bear, and how many lives would be spared or ruined by a mad man, whom ego had no boundaries and conscious only bared hate and selfishness. Maybe I was being bias, angry or simply telling the damn truth the way I saw it, and the way it was, it was my story and it is based on what I witnessed with the many American soldiers who saw it the way I did. It was hell and I am entitled to tell it the way my perception, experience and opinion lived it. My thoughts were one of them was never going to see again, and the other might never walk. As I walked home that morning, I could not think on more tragedy to come, but I knew I had to be strong in order to be effective. It was hard sometimes for me to separate my emotions from life's struggle right before my eyes and hands. I could only imagine the soldiers that were not fortunate as the soldiers that lives had already been snuffed out because of greed, a sick leader, egotistic maniac, and a horror of hell. This was not familiar to me, it was all to me the television sitcom MASH, it was not a play story before my eyes, but this story was real. There wasn't any staging or actors. At one point, I felt helpless there was not much I could do, other than my trained nursing expertise's. I wanted to scream, because I wanted so much to replace those eyes and restore the functions of those legs, but this was reality, it wasn't going to happen unless a miracle from God was going to take place and that was inevitable.

I was not hungry, all I wanted to do was sleep, because I knew if I slept, then I was able to think consciously and the pain I felt would be eliminated only by dreams of being conscious. It seemed almost a ritual to be stressed out, but sleep would secure all. I guess that seemed like the thing to do, because it was hell trying to escape, since it was already coded in my mind. I could only think of the Vietnam soldiers again, serving the war, later diagnosed with having post traumatic stress disorders. I only prayed that I would be spared such a disease that in reality was only looked upon as still a mental instability. As I cuddled and zipped myself, as I did every night with a blanket, sweat suits, and zippered my sleeping bag from head to toe, I tonight thought of home. My heart began to palpitate as I wished I could be home with my family. Only then did I begin to understand the torment my buddy was going through. She had already missed home so bad that it was beginning to show on her, and she looked as if she had aged twice her age since we first met. As I wiggled from under my sleeping bag, perspiration drenched my body and clothes. I was hot, lonely, and most of the times, up too early, but I was use to getting up an hour or two earlier than the rest, since I enjoyed walking the terrain and brushing my teeth in peace in search to find solitude. I often would take the time out to look to be with my Father in heaven alone, and look up at the sky and enjoy the sunrise as it slowly engulfs the sky as always; so beautiful. I would allow myself to escape with my silent thoughts as the rainbow rays of color emerged with the sun and began a new day.

Many of the Medical troops positioned themselves as they anxiously awaited the Medics to bring in the wounded. The tension was too high, and our faces expressed uncertainty as we all silently awaited the receiving of the many casualties. I was in shock but knew I had to do what I was taught to do. As two of the MP's (military police) approached the doors and swung them opened, the medics, and some of the medical staff, including myself hurriedly rushed to the truck to unload and assist in the removal of the gurney's of the many wounded.

Once we entered the emergency room where the doctors and the rest of the medical staff were we began to assess them. I noticed the torn limbs and the torn ligaments, the blood was overwhelming as the soldiers moaned in distress while we attempted and continued to prepare them for surgery. The emergency room was chaotic, there were soldiers everywhere. Medical soldiers scattered in different directions for supplies that were kept in their various places. As I looked down I noticed the blood drenched clothing soaking through the man-made floor of plastic, while the footprints of boot soles and streaks of blood stained the floor. The smell of fresh blood and the trauma of it all invaded my nostrils and I became nauseated. I wanted to vomit but I knew I had to hold my feelings and myself together because the wounded and my staff needed me to function above the normalcy of my human capabilities . . . but I was a human being.

Gurney's polluted the emergency room, while some soldiers lay in wait for treatment. There were too many to care for; too many to service at the same time, even though we had several doctors. The urgent care patients were immediately treated and seen to; but to me they all were emergencies; however, the ones that would not survive were seen last because that was the rule, the policies of the Army (SOP-Standards Operational Procedures) and we had to follow the order of care.

I started to approach a gurney that laid an Iraqi soldier covered with blood, his mangled body lay dormant and destroyed by grenades, but before I could do anything the Chaplain covered his body as I approached him, as I watched the blood seeped through the sheet after he was given his last rites. I felt helpless because I was unable to help him and although he was an Iraqi he was still a human being, somebody's loved one, but his body remained there, still, until they took him to the morgue.

There were many nights like this, but you never get use to the blood, the guts and the destruction of what war can do to another human being . . . yet I continued to function as a nurse and as a soldier. One night as my staff and I quietly attended to our patients on our unit, a phone call interrupted and requested that another nurse and I report to the emergency room . . . . I knew it was the beginning of so many nights of injured soldiers including our own U.S. fatalities. It was as usual, a night of chaos.

As we always had to keep ourselves prepared in position as we waited and heard the motors of the trucks approaching, we saw two MP's approach, but this time I stood back and allow the others to unload the casualties.

When my patient approached the gurney his body was a mess, his bloody face was distorted and his skin was torn and jagged as his cries gave in to the suffering and pain as his legs plummet over the gurney lifeless while the blood dripped onto the floor; his bones and flesh of chunky red beef was exposed. Gently, I lifted his leg back onto the gurney while cries of his pain echoed the emergency room. His clothing was stripped and was of non-uniform (he was an Iraqi soldier-but was not dressed in uniform. Just like many, he was a civilian forced to fight) His bare feet told the story of injuries, they too were bloody.

I initiated IV (intravenous fluids), while others drew blood and the doctor assessed him, and prepared him for X-rays and surgery.

When I walked back to my unit this thought wouldn't leave my mind . . . I could not help think that we all could be infected because none of us wore protective gloves, but that thought quickly subsided because the awareness for gloves was not expound on when you're dealing with urgent alarms for assistance.

There were many times I would walk the hospital and visit the other ICU's where many injured soldiers were laid, with faces and limbs bandaged looking mummified. The reality of war had finally begun to sink in.

Some times we would mingle with the other troops in the eating tents, but some times it was difficult to find seating since most of the times it was overcrowded. I would usually boil water in a metal solid basin that I had cherished deeply and would wash right there in my tent. My tent was weird. I had several lesbians right under my nose, not to mention the Captain who slept right next to me, who was built like a man, very muscular as if she lifted weights twenty-four seven. Some were even lovers and slept very close together. The female tent was housed with officers. I did not see a problem in their preference, but I knew that it was unpleasing to God, since he says, "It is a sin to be lovers of the same sex, and those who are disobedient would burn in brimstone and fire." Everyone knew of some of their preference, because it was obvious in their behavior that they really didn't care who knew, not to mention the one who acted more masculine than the other ones. As long as they stayed their distance, I frankly did not care what they did, since my philosophy is to each is own. Although I felt the captain had some attraction for me, since she always found something to reprimand my buddy and myself with. Nothing that would get us into major trouble, just simple stuff like, no smoking in the tent, etc., although she never seen us, she just assumed we did since we both were smokers. One day, I thought she had lost her rockers. After having one of the Sergeants kindly, put up a partition and built me some cardboard drawers, I was lying in my bed, putting sand in little Tabasco bottle, so I could have them for souvenirs when I returned back home. I knew she was in the tent, because she always made a lot of noise rearranging her belongings and using her kettle for hot water. The noise did not bother me as much since the tent always seemed busy with traffic in and out, and the echo of female voices throughout the tent. Our tent was a new MGP (medium size tent) that had approximately 16-20 female officers who occupied it. I can remember the disgust and frustration on my buddy's face when we first move in because the female next to her wanted to overtake her space, leaving her very little room for her belongings. She was so frustrated and aggravated about it, she told her in a nice way by taking enough space that was due her. You see, my buddy was not all overbearing as most people have defined me as, but there are times when you have to be or people would simply take advantage of you. So, I applauded her action with a "let's go and smoke a cigarette." Of course the officer was upset because she knew that she was wrong, so she pouted for a few days, but eventually subdued and made the best out of a bad situation. As for Weenie, she was never really bothered by it, but that situation only encouraged her more to think about going home. Although she tried at times to act brave, I could look into her eyes and see the sadness in them, but I did not know how to reach her. So, I continued to pray for her as I did day and night for the unit, the country, and myself.

Getting back to the Captain, I later bathed in my tent until the unit could provide us with man-made showers that worked. As I stood in my birthday suit, (naked), the Captain next to me pushed open the shower curtains I had up for a partition and just stood there. I stood there speechless with my mouth wide open; I could not believe what had happened. She did not say anything before she invaded my privacy. She just stood there, her eyes looking at me in lust. When I finally got over being shock and mostly embarrassed, she blurted out, "oh I am sorry." That really frightened me. I was afraid to sleep or be in the tent alone after that happened. I did not know what to expect from her. I thought crazy thoughts of her attacking me, if she caught me alone, but of course, it was just my imagination, and I never placed myself in a position to be alone. I hurried and bathed quickly and waited for my buddy to finish bathing, so I could rat on that big fish. After all, she was a Captain, and I was always told higher rank had its privileges. In that respect I kept it to myself, other than telling Weenie; and in that case what could they do to her if I did make a noise, probably nothing, and she could always reply, "I didn't know she was undressing." When my buddy finished bathing, we went for a walk and discuss what had happened to calm our nerves. I enjoyed having a buddy like Weenie; we had so much in common. We could talk to each other and give each other support. When we returned, the lights were out and Weenie went to sleep, but as for me praying and listening to CNN was my way of keeping my sanity. It was extremely cold that night, more so than the others, although I though I was bundled appropriately, I was cold shortly after.

I was awakened by the noise static of CNN that had just gone off the air. "Oh what a pity". To me CNN was my only hope and reality I had left of the real world; something I could hold on to, knowing the world still exist. Although most of the information was of the war, I was being updated of what was actually going on around me; the news of Israel, Jordan, and other Arab countries were the most priority. Scud missiles were being intercepted by our patriots and the continuation of Saddam psychotic malicious behavior. Some times when I awaken at night, I would lie in my bed in deep thought. I had to pinch myself at times, so I could know, this was not a bad dream, it was real. I begin to think of the young men and women who fought in Vietnam and what strategy they used and how they felt, when they awakened only to hear: the sand hitting the tents, the ricocheting effects of the bombing, the soft echoes of the wind, and the starling frightened faces of their peers. I would often look at those who were sleeping until I fell asleep myself, since there was nothing at that time of hour to do. Sometimes I would think of my family and try to figure out the time of day it was in Florida, and what they were doing at that particular hour, until I drifted off into never land. I heard a soft whispered voice calling, Beanie, Beanie, wake up. I had over slept; I guess I was over tired that morning, since I'm usually the first person up in the tent. The format was the same, the usual formation, gathering together, and breakfast (if you wanted to indulge), and back to work, so much for having a day off. The hospital was looking good. Our ward master was neat and had a great sense of humor. He was knowledgeable, and he knew exactly what was needed to run our ICW. My Head nurse was also knowledgeable and did not have any problems working hard. I was appointed the OIC (officer in charge) of our section, which included (three to four 91 Charleys'), (two Bravos'), and three to four nurses.

Destroyed Iraqi Trucks

Iraqi prisoners all fatally wounded shortly after take off

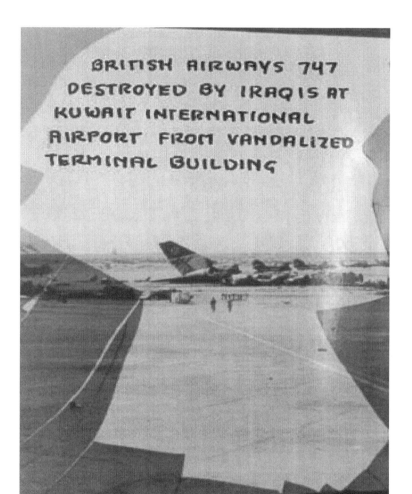

Chapter 15

War Gossip Or Simply Just Rumours?

I must have drifted off to sleep, because the next thing I knew mid evening had approached. I felt good today for some reason; only if I knew why? I felt I had extra energy, since most of the times I was dragging my feet. Today I wanted to feel special too, but I didn't have any perfume to enhance those special feelings. After a hardy dinner, I chatted with Weenie, as we always did, we chatted about everything and everybody. We had a unique relationship. Although, we had recently met, it seemed as though we knew each other for years. Weenie was a laid back individual, sincere, humble, but she did not allow anyone to walk over her. She was short in statue, young middle age, but her demeanor was of a tall powerful Amazon. She was special, but most of all, she was my buddy, my friend my confidant. She wasn't much for idle gossip, but she was concerned like myself with the behavior some of the troops were displaying. Some of the soldiers had forgotten their commitments and vows, and they were in heat like a dog on a prowl. One day, while I was in the tent, a few friends visited the compound to retrieve the rest of the equipment they had left behind. At that time I received a hand-written letter from one of the soldier that relocated with the original unit at another location in the desert. The letter stated, that the chief nurse (a colonel) got caught having sex with a Captain on a Five-ton, while a soldier was making rounds on KP duty. I was flabbergasted, and astonished about the disturbing news. Most of all, I was disappointed because I had regarded her as my role model. She was stern, professional, and full of wealth of military knowledge; but I understood the human nature, and she was also a human being underneath that tough exterior. I was disappointed by her behavior, and her inability to make the right choice, too many had expected this type of behavior, and it is most expected for any black leader holding a high position unfortunately. Although it happened, the damage was done, it was a slap in the face for the standards of the military codes and ethics, and her leadership abilities will now be questioned. I was disappointed that her decision was not discreet. My reason for saying this is, when we were mobilized back in the United States, she made such a big fuss over the officers having men in their barracks, even if they were our husbands. Now she was cohabiting with a Captain and had been seen coming out of an ISO (army operating room) very early in the morning along with him, that behavior was not acceptable. I really can't express the hurt and betrayal I felt. Although I was not with them, the person who told the story was indeed honest and had said nothing added in other than the truth. Everyone seemed to discuss the recent gossip with snickering and laughter. She was the topic for the remainder of the day and the days that follow.

The lines were always too long, but today I was lucky; I was able to get my food with little to no wait. When I did eat breakfast, which was rare, I would eat in the recreation tent along with the others. It was always impossible to really enjoy your meals there, since the tent was small, overcrowded, noisy, and almost impossible to converse, but this was home away from home, my AO: (my space), along with so many others. This was a good day to wash my clothing and let the sunrays beam them dry and that is exactly what I did besides, write a few letters home and rest up for my usual work at 7 p.m. When I arrived to work, talk was already circulating that POWs (prisoners of war) were in ICU and in critical condition and in other wards. Myself being curious of whom these people were, I decided to visit the other wards to see for myself. It was horrified to see, those poor mange bodies laying there helplessly, attached to monitors and tubes, in hopes of keeping them alive or to save what was left. As I walked through the tent of ICU, I could barely see some of their faces, let alone their entirety, since bandages embraced their wounds. It was hard for me to accept or justify my concerns and compassion, since these were the enemies; they were dangerous, but the human side would not allow me to ponder any hostility, after all, they were human beings too. I felt chills throughout my body and thought this could have been me. There I go again having empathy, but should there be compassion for the enemy? According to the Geneva Convention we should be compassionate towards one another but are they? In reality, we were no better than they were since we were there to defend a country that was not a part of America, so why have compassion for either side? I flashed back to those soldiers of earlier wars; did they have compassion for the enemies when they came face to face with death? So my compassion for them left, but my responsibility and my mission to provide the best nursing skills was always in focus. Why was I questioning myself and feeling sorry for someone who didn't know me or my platoon or gave a damn about me; maybe some might have, after all, some were forced in this war, whether they liked it or not. Most of them had on civilian attire and most of them had on sandals. How a real leader could send troops with inadequate clothing to fight a war, I don't know. War is usually planned, negotiated and would have their men well equipped, all these soldiers had were themselves, AK-47, and fear all over their faces. As I walked back to the ward, I felt loneliness inside. I felt empty, helpless, and saddened by the disasters that created a war, but I knew I had to be strong in order to survive, because I knew one day, I would be whole again. I prayed forgiveness for allowing myself to question my compassion. The night went fairly quickly and I walked towards my tent while the sunrays lay against my back. I dragged myself inside and lay on my cot, and quickly glanced to my friend's space that soon would be empty. Suddenly, I felt a rush of loneliness within my soul. As I lay there for a while, reminiscing about home, and how beautiful it would be to see my children smile again and how desperately I needed at that moment for my husband to hold me and reassure me that soon the war would be over. It was neat to be many miles away and imagine home, as if home and my family were right before me. It was as if I could actually see and touch them and insist on a hug. It was amazing to visualize in your mind, as if they were actually before me, how fascinating the mind was. I placed my headphones on, as I did every time before I went to bed, the only thing that disturbed me was the horrors of the war progressing, but my ritual continued. Listening to CNN kept me alive and informed me of what was going on around me. The longer I sat there, trying to listen to my favorite station, my tired body insisted on sleep, so I decided to do my usual ritual, heat some water on the kerosene heater, and sponged off. Our new plywood sheets manmade shower stalls were almost ready, but that morning, they were not in operation. I sipped some hot cocoa, which became my favorite over tea, and snuggled myself beneath the covers hoping to get some sleep. It was hard, most of the time, to sleep, since unusual noises and traffic sometimes disturbed me.

Chapter 16

Departing Friendship

Today was not an ordinary day, something sad was happening, Weenie my closet confidant was leaving. Weenie had talked about home regularly, and now her sad eyes no longer showed fear and despair, today it showed a sign of relief. For me, it was one of the saddest days of my life; my buddy was departing, going home. One side of me wanted to rejoice because I knew this had been a long dream for her to come true, but there was also one side of me, who wanted her to stay, so I would not be alone. I don't mean to sound selfish, but I have learned to trust her so much. We had so much in common, a family, and much idle conversation. She was awesome, we could talk for hours without being argumentative or bored, but today, she was leaving me all alone. At least I felt all-alone. I wanted to scream as she packed carefully, not forgetting anything, as I helped her along, wishing something could happen, not to separate our friendship. As she packed, she offered items and belongings that may be useful to me. We exchanged addresses and talked about visiting each other when the war was over. I was beginning to miss her already, but I knew she desperately needed to be home with her family, especially her daughter and grandchild, who needed her more than I. We laughed about the silly things that day, but for the most part, we were much quieter than we usually had been. When we were not working, we were inseparable, always together, laughing, smoking, and walking the desert. We even visited the latrines together while one kept watch as usual, but this unity was about to dissolve as if death was knocking. I could only express my sadness for her and how much I would miss her and for her to keep in touch and to write me. She too had sad words of farewell enchantment and how she would keep in touch and visit me once the war was over. We talked as she packed, and I fought very hard to hold back the tears, because I did not want her to worry. Red Cross had sent her papers and the General had given her the okay to leave. A Five-ton truck was picking her up late that afternoon and I would have the pleasure of seeing her off. Weenie never told me exactly what was going on at home, other than her daughter and grandchild was having problems. I don't think she didn't trust me, probably what I would think of her situation. I assume she felt embarrassed and didn't know how I would handle her problem. So she played it safe and kept the problem to herself. It really didn't matter what the problem was, as long as she could resolve it when she returned home, and I anticipated everything would work out fine for her. Her side became empty as if no one ever slept there, but it allowed me to move my belonging a little wider, but the soldier next to her felt the same way. It was about that time and Weenie was ready to leave, so I helped her with her belongings, duffel bag and all to the destination where she would meet the truck, that would send her to her fulfilled awaited dream. We were early, so we embraced; shed some tears, as we waited for the Five-ton truck to pick her up. As I watched the truck leave, I could barely see it as it vanished out of sight, leaving clouds of sand dust and traces of tires in the terrain. I felt totally isolated and all alone as if I was left behind. I felt as if I was the only one in the desert. I cried as I walked back to the tent. From that day, it was never the same, I always felt I was missing something, our bond that was so special was broken and I often wonder if I would see her again. I often answered questions of what happened to "Captain Weenie", most of the time unanswered, because I didn't know exactly what really happened to her, only my suspicious speculations.

 Days would pass and my soul was filled with emptiness, and my feelings of loneliness were evident. It was to hard to adjust myself being alone, since I was so use to talking to Weenie almost daily, and now the only one I had left to talk to was God. I knew these feelings of sadness would pass, as the days would follow, but I needed to allow myself to feel the loss and redirect, myself, and focus my thoughts on what was happening around me, that in time, the isolation would ease, and I would function in normalcy again. Until that time could take place, I felt the void, despair and loneliness, and the longing of a friend, I stood alone.

Chapter 17

Mail Call, The Forgotten Soldier

Our usual daily activities didn't change much. We were operational and in full force at the hospital. The weather began to get lousy, rain, sandstorms, but maybe it was always lousy and I was too busy to pay it much attention. I became familiar with sandstorms that overpowered the hospital as if it had a mission of its own. The winds were high and fierce and you could hear the beating of the sand against the tents. Rain began to take its toll, but because of the extreme heat, we worshiped the outpour that allowed us to cool off for a short while. Mail call was its usual time, and as always I waited patiently with the crowd to hear my name call, but as usual, my name was never called, leaving me puzzled and disappointed. "Why was I not receiving any mail I thought", since I had family back home, and I had written to so many people, I looked forward to the caring in return, yet I continued to stand in the crowded midst of the many soldiers, hoping to get just a postcard from anybody, but yet nothing. Maybe it was the constant relocations were to blame why I never received much mail or shall I say received any. I finally accepted the fact that the frequent relocations were the reason I was not receiving any mail, but I thought no one had time to write to me.

Chapter 18

"Cease Fire", The War Is Over

Tonight at work was rambunctious. It seemed like everyone was in an exceptionally good mood. Our patients were making progress, cheerful and talkative. We had completed our routine nursing assessment on our patients, administered their medications, and sat down to relax as downtime permitted. We turned on the news and huddled by the nurses' station, when a special announcement aired the station, stating the Air Force Base in Dhahran has just been hit by Saddam's soldiers, and several officers have been killed instantly. As our eyes looked on each other in amazement and shock, I could not help wondering; that it could have been one of us. A long pause of silence went by and a sense of frustration rang the room. I could not help but wonder about their families and loved ones, and the senseless grief this war has caused. Our joyful faces no longer had smiles on them; they had turned into faces of despair. When was this war ending? How many more lives had to be sacrificed? If I could only answer this question, then I too would be considered a hero or had a genius with a high IQ or had psychic abilities. As we regained all composure, the news continued to say these Air Force officers that died minutes ago had just arrived in Saudi. I wondered did they know their fate. It was all too real. It could not have been happening. I was just dreaming and I was about to wake up and the war would be forever gone, but I was in Saudi, officers were killed, and I was not dreaming. My thought could only focus on how hideous and sickened this man's mind must have been and how the U.S. had to stop him before more disasters and lives were taken. Our patients became quieter as if disbelief had sat in, but you could see the looks on their faces had spelled sadness. As the news continued, a reporter haughty voice chanted out that Saddam has ordered "cease fire". The war was over. As we jumped up and down to the good news, we could not erase the fact that minutes before, officers and soldiers lives had been lost. The room became quiet again, because we were not sure if this was one of Saddam prank to relax us while he attacked elsewhere. Until our leader confirmed it, the war to us was not over. Other soldiers rushed through the wards, chanting the war is over, the war is over. Saddam has ordered cease-fire with huge vows of relief across their faces. But I was not buying into Saddam's game, I wanted to hear it from my commander that cease-fire was actually in effect. Saddam was definitely an individual you could not trust. In my opinion, he was less than human, non-compassionate, cold, ruthless, a immortal human being. How on earth could anyone trust a person as careless and untruthful as who would trust a black widow spider. Our ears grew close to the radio as we listened to the news, cease-fire was initiated and a sense of sadness, relief, and joy had empowered us. Yet we were not set free to return to our families. I could not help to think how bless I was to be alive and how I was not going to be shipped home in some body bag. When was the war ending? Happiness engulfed me because my family was not going to experience such grief or loss, I thought. I prayed and thanked Jesus along with the others for our lives. I was actually coming home alive. But I could not help to wonder about their families loved ones and the senseless grief this war had caused. Our joyful faces no longer had smiles on them instead they had turned into faces of sorrow. How can a family member prepare themselves for the death of a love one and how would they react when they are told a love one was not returning? In a sense it was a humanitarian mission completed that has caused so much suffering and so much grief. I began to really pray to my Father for allowing my life to be spared and how thankful I was to be alive to return home to my family. I quickly imagined Weenie's face how it would have glowed if she were here, but I could not help imagine how safe she was at home, and then I silently asked myself before wanted to know when were we leaving? Morning seemed as if it was never going to come, but when it did I found myself walking slowly to my tent without a heavy burden on my back. Cease-fire had allowed me to relax a little, even if it was for a moment, I was going to enjoy it and feel somewhat free.

Chapter 19

"At Ease"

Operational Desert Storm was over and our wards were full of enemies at our hospital. You could see the relief in the soldier's faces as we greeted each other as we passed. You could almost feel the weight that was lifted as if it suspended itself in the air, as if power was removed from our body. I felt like I could shout like the Sunday church folks do when the Holy Spirit take control, (lost in the spirit, anointed of the Holy Ghost, spirit dancing) excited about the end of the war, I too was excited. I could remember myself thanking God several times again as if my inner spirit knew something more than I did. The war was over, but was it really? I waited for the final word to come; time was definitely on my side. The only thing that was in operation was to dismantle the hospital and inventory it. I knew that once I participated in taking the hospital down, I knew I was closer to seeing my family again. It was actually almost over. I could only think back to that morning February 14, 1991, when I was ill and my heart felt as if it was going to crush into pieces. It was Valentine's Day and I was sick and my sweetheart was no where close to comfort me. I went on sick call, saw the doctor, had some x-rays done, that mimic possible pneumonia. My lungs were blackened, probably from the black soot that came from the kerosene heaters or the environment that I resided in. I was given medications, including a Depo-Provera injection, that prevented me from menstruating, which I thought was a good idea, since problems with sanitation was not a high regard. At that time, I thought I was never going to get better. Since every time I would blow my nose, my tissue would be covered with black soot from the machinery that surrounded and kerosene heaters that was used to keep us warm. I thought I had contracted some foreign disease. Although there were many hard times, the war was finally over, and I was going home.

Unfortunately, I didn't get quarters that day, so I had to return to work the next day, but I thank God for allowing me to just have that. It seemed like years had passed and time was at a stand still and everyone and everything seems to move in slow motion. I guess I expected to see much happier faces. Constant hugs that embraced were the sign of relief on their faces and the warmth was felt, but there was not much of that. Formation was scheduled and we were given briefing of what was happening and what to expect next. Our main concern was to get those people who were hospitalized back to CONUS (United States) or the Evac hospital. That mission did not seem too hard. It did not take us long to get those casualties out of the hospital into their rightful places where they belong.

A few days had gone by and I finally had some time to write my family. I told them what was happening and updated them on everything that was going on. For the first time since I'd been in Saudi Arabia, I had a strong feeling of missing my children, a burning sensation wanting so much to go home. You see, my children have always been the center of my survival in my life and my constant struggle to make things better for them. I longed and I wanted to embrace them. Anticipation marked the faces of those who were of the 31st CASH hospital out of Germany. Rumor had it; we would be detached and returned to our original unit, just like those casualties. There was much hostility, frustration, and despair for most of us because we didn't want to return. Speaking for the group, I don't think that it had anything to do with personalities; it was 31st CASH had become our family and we were use to them. Our unit didn't show much regard when they left us in the desert, homeless and without the necessities that we might had needed. Remembering how our unit departed, our unit didn't seem to show much caring, but the unit we were attached to made us feel welcome. Many thoughts arose, why should we go back to a unit who got lost for almost four months in the desert without accomplishing their mission. Getting reattached was going to happen, no matter what they thought. It was only a few days that would quickly pass us by, before we would be reattached and reunited with our unit. I guess it wasn't too bad after all. It really didn't matter to me who, and what they thought, as long as being reattached meant I was closer to home and being reunited with my family. Word had got around the compound and before long; everyone knew our hidden desires that we wanted to stay with them until it was time to go home.

The 31st CASH wanted to do something special for the troops, so they decided to cook us a barbecue bash. Besides, it was also in lieu of Black history month. We had various poem readings that week. We also put on a black talent show. The planning went smoothly, but the preparations were tough, after all there were no Aunt Jemima in the kitchen. We must have brought and cleaned about twenty dozen of chickens, yes actually cleaned them. We had so many potatoes for potato salad, I just couldn't believe we peeled them all, and one of our soldiers made their famous barbecue sauce. We cooked and barbecue all day long and by the time the food was done most of the preparers weren't really hungry. We had music and soldiers from all over stroll by to feast. It was awesome, but I certainly wouldn't want to do it again no time soon.

We were definitely one big happy family and I was glad we were. The thought of leaving them, still lingered, how they would be missed.

My sleeping arrangements were made along with a partition to provide privacy. My area was a small cubicle, approximately 10 x 4 feet, but it was livable, home away from home. Although I didn't have much room, I was glad to have found friendship again and a place to sleep; who could ask for much more, after all no one else seems to show much concern. There wasn't a whole lot to do, so I felt myself walking around the compound familiarizing myself of my surroundings. There was not much change in our location, and the claustrophobia of dusty sand tent clustered together. As I walked back towards my tent, I noticed the stars above me. I thought if only I could take one of them and send a message to my family, I would let them know I was okay, and how happy I would be, if I could be with them again.

When I returned to my tent, I found my space and chatted with one of the soldier. The conversation was of little speech since I was tired, I wanted to retire. It was too late to take a shower, so again, my usual routine of boiling water on the kerosene heater, and washing off in my little room that had a partition. When all was completed, I nestled in my sleeping bag, zipped myself from head to toe as I did every night. The temperature would drop drastically low and it would be very cold. I placed my headphones on and listened to gospel, and in between songs, I prayed until sleep somehow took control. Morning came too sudden and my feet had felt as if it they had traveled on rugged rock. I was endlessly tired, but I had to attend formation. I assumed my daily ritual as I did most morning and headed for chow. The lines were long as usual and the food was of course, lousy. And tasted of no nutritional value or if there was any nutritional value, and there certainly wasn't any, when the food reached your plate. But, I was thankful to have exerted myself with only a bowl of cereal and a lukewarm container of milk. I might sound as if I am complaining, but the truth of the matter was, I was grateful to eat it. For that quick moment, I thought about God and was grateful he had spared my life. I guess I allowed myself at times to become selfish, that I didn't think about His blessings He had allowed me. Formation was hot, and I couldn't believe we were required to dress in full gear, (with helmet, belt and suspenders), which seemed so ridiculous since the war was over. Full gear would be appropriate having no say to the military ways, you get use to then and cope with them, instead of questioning their rationale, if you wanted to remain sane or career oriented. It would not have been so bad if formation was brief, but it usually dragged on while the sun baked your body and beads of perspiration sweep down your face causing fresh newly make up to streak also. Oh what a sight. When formation was dismissed, there was talk about going into town. I could not have been so elated on my new venture, since there was nothing to do but inventory medical equipment that never was opened, but it seemed as though this was a man made ritual, to pass time to keep us busy and occupied. I found myself on back of a Five-ton enjoying the sights as we rode through town. Sometimes you could see the ruins the war had caused, burned buildings, tankers and aircrafts. Those Saudi folks were crazy. They drove as if they were never going to reach their destination. They weaned in and out of traffic as if no other cars were on the road. Until my observation, all the cars were white. I never understood why, but every car or truck I saw was either a Toyota or white, not to mention, filthy, dirty, as if water never touched them. I also noticed that the women sat in the back seat of a car, while the men and little boys sat up front. That was the Middle East customs; women were not regarded much as individuals in their culture. They were strictly there for reproduction. When you see the limited liberation these women had, we definitely would not survive long in that culture. Not to mention the Pakistanis they were not allowed to practice their religion. We journeyed through the narrow streets; I could not help notice a group of children and women with torn, shabby, dusty clothes on attending to the sheep that were also dirty. The town looked empty as to refer to it as the ghost town, but there were people living there. The houses were covered and surrounded by layers of brick that almost made the houses very invisible. We finally approached KKMC gates, with soldiers at each door of the Five-ton requesting identification, to see if we were legitimate. The gates opened and we were signaled to enter. As we entered, I was amazed to see beautiful planted color flowers embedded in the soil and palm trees. As we drove further, you could see the beautiful symbol of Saudi. A brass symbol palm tree encased inside a circular ring shape. The streets were clean and it looked as if we had entered into another world all by itself. For the first time, I was able to witness greenery, not much, but enough to make me think I was elsewhere other than Saudi Arabia desert. We came upon a big building looking like a warehouse. There was U.S. soldiers everywhere, as if this was the meeting place of the town. Everyone was here and boy was it crowded. We jumped off the Five-ton and dispersed in our separate ways after quickly being brief and where we would meet when we were finished doing whatever we needed to do. When I entered this huge warehouse, I was asked to show military identification. The place was tremendously large. I didn't know what direction I wanted to go in first. They had everything from batteries, food, to hair relaxers. I thought about buying one, but who was going to take a chance in perming their hair in the desert? I knew my hair needed a new looked but I wasn't going to take any chance; even though my hair felt like brillo and was starting to turn green from the black dye I had put in it prior to leaving the United States. There was so many items, boxes upon boxes, and the entire place was crowded with soldiers trying to stock up on can goods, just in case. I myself bought a few can goods, Vienna sausages, and other snacks. The checks out lines were long, but it seemed as though they went fast and the wait was not as long as I expected. I left there and found myself on the telephone line that was around the corner from the warehouse with lots of barbwire on fences surrounding it. The lines there were just as long, but this time I didn't take 2-3 hours to use them, just approximately almost 20-25 minutes. I finally stroll myself right to the entrance. It was my turn and about four others as they counted us inside.

Inside was dark and gloomy, these telephones inside the building were similar to the others, dark and gloomy, but they were more comfortable, because they allowed us little stools to sit on while you talked instead of standing. Of course, you were not given a whole lot of time to chat, approximately 15-20 minutes; you were given a minute lecture prior to making your call and soldiers walked up and down the aisle to ensure you were doing it properly or for what other reasons they had. I called home and chatted to my husband, only to be told some distressing news, my first cousin had died after an elective operation. I was stunned and fought very hard to hold back the tears, but no matter how hard I tried a few rolled down my face anyway. My entire day was ruined; I could not help thinking on why it happened? I then became angry at my husband because the last thing I needed was this, but it was too late, he had already wrecked my day. I thought of her throughout the day, her smile, her undying strength to be independent and her willingness not to be selfish, I will miss her. This added to my clouded emotions, my friend Weenie has left me and now my cousin is no longer a part of this world. Who will I visit when I return to North Carolina? It will never be the same again. I reminisce on the days that I did visit, how much fun we would have and how much food she would consume. She loved to eat and I didn't make it easier. I knew I had to place this emotion deep within my heart; there were too many things to worry about, the possibility of war happening again, the wait, and going home. The good news was the children were okay and they missed me terribly. After leaving the warehouse, we went to the shopping mall. It was small and lovely. There weren't too many stores and the only stores I saw were the jewelry shop, a grocery, a restaurant, and a shopping store. There were a few sights to see. I first went into the grocery store and it was crowded as well. To my amazement, I didn't see any Arabic women; just men and their children, not to mention their mannerism were rude of the men, but probably accepted within our culture. After I had found the necessary items I wished to purchase, I stood in line, as I normally did. When all of a sudden this Arabic man, briskly jumped in front of me, pushed me off balance and placed his things on the counter. There were no excuses or apologies rendered, just bold-face rudeness in our culture as it would be called in our culture. I couldn't believe it, but this seemed to be the norm in their culture. This took me back remembering the time the Arabic man had coffee and only offered some to the men, but not the women, when we were lost in the desert and came upon a store. Women simply were not regarded as equal, if they were regarded at all. I certainly was in for a rude awakening, if I had to live in this country. After my first encounter adventure, I walked across to the other side, which was really far apart and found myself inside this large shopping store. I browsed around and said hello to a few other soldiers I knew and found myself as usual in the perfume section. The fragrances were unique; their perfumes are simply made from oil and they smell so natural. The perfume gave off a certain aura that seemed to attract people of either sex; I brought a few for family and friends. I stayed away from buying American made apparel, only because I can get them back home anytime. We left there and made our way into the jewelry store, it was awfully crowded, body to body contact. It was not visible to see anything in the counters, because army green fatigue blocked your vision. Once our journey was completed, we were headed back to the compound. Everyone seemed somewhat contented since we all had a chance to unwind. As we journeyed back, nightfall was approaching and it was very hard to see my site as we did when we first ventured off. We finally arrived to the compound tired and ready for bed, and of course to a new day. Now that I had the opportunity to escape and find solitude, I was sure I would return. Having had the opportunity to escape, I found new peace heading into town. This became my ritual any time I heard of anyone going into town, I was sure to find myself right along with them. Money was becoming scarce, so I was told where I could go to get up to fifty dollars in advance pay and didn't have to pay it back until I returned to the United States. This loaning of monies was down by the military base and it became a known fact to most soldiers when they needed funds. This offer was good because, if you didn't have money this was a great opportunity to have some and repay the military later once you returned to the United States. Now that I was a shopping fanatic, I just had something else to do, something energizing, instead of walking, running, and thinking desert. Some of the soldiers, mostly young ones, were putting on a fashion show. They gathered and worked in separate places around the compound sewing and preparing for it. Unfortunately, I was on the Five-ton headed for town. I enjoyed these moments so much better, having the opportunity to call home, eat, and shop. Although I didn't get the chance to see the fashion show, I heard that it was very nice. When I returned, it was late, and all I wanted to do was to shower, find my cot, and rest. I smothered myself between the wool blanket and sleeping bag, and placed my headsets on and listened to CNN. Before I knew it, morning had approached and formation was scheduled at its usual time, too early.

Chapter 20

"Palm Sunday"

It was only a few days to Palm Sunday and I wanted very much to attend service. The Assistant Chaplain had met a preacher from another unit who would be conducting services on Sunday. The Assistant Chaplain had provided us with service during the week, Bible study, and on Friday, "Saints Night." I would attend because I loved to hear the sermon on God and his Son, Jesus. They were uplifting and you had a sense of belonging and of course, there really wasn't much to do. Palm Sunday was beautiful, everyone ran out of their tents to watch the sunrise. It was beautiful, almost like a sparkling rainbow, but was radiant as your eyes gleamed. Service was held at another unit. It was approximately about 3-4 miles away. We didn't have transportation, so we had to foot it across the compound in full gear, since that was the military protocol. We filled our canteen with water and walked across. It was a few of us, including my non-religion roommate that went. The day was beautiful, but it was extremely hot, perspiration poured down our faces before we could reach our one-mile mark, some of us stopped to sip on some water and dry our faces before we could proceed again. One thing about the desert, so many things seems so close, but yet, they were very far off. We continued our journey, sometimes we would jog, and sometimes we would kick the sand as if we were fulfilling one of our childhood plays, but all in all, we were having fun. I held my Bible tight so I would not drop it in the sand. The Chaplain said that we were almost there, but then she said that a mile ago. Maybe we were close, because we came upon a mounted roll of sand with wire in a circular position and a group of soldiers. The Chaplain told them where we were going and gave them the password and they allowed us to enter. As we made our entrance into the compound, it seemed as if we had to climb up mountains of sand piles that seemed almost like a hill, and then climb down again. It was rough, but we were determined to be in church. After walking a quarter of a mile, we came upon some tents.

The unit looked organized; the tents were neatly arranged in a row. We finally found the tent where services were being held, but it was confusing because there were two tents that offered different religious services. The outside had its insigma and the surrounding looked neat. As we entered the tent, we were greeted at the entrance politely and welcomed in. The chairs were neatly arranged and the center of the pulpit was decorated for Palm Sunday and the center table had communion neatly laid out and covered to signify its purity. I found a seat and waited for the service to began. I was welcomed again before the sermon took place. We sang hymns and had prayer and for those who desired communion were able to come forward in an organized fashion. When Church was over, we greeted each other and was given a piece of palm as we exited the Church. The service was beautiful and uplifting. You came unknowing, but left feeling renewed in spirit. We ventured across the compound to our unit, but this time, the distance didn't seem that long. Nothing was happening back at the unit, secret lovers trying to be discreet, soldiers laying out trying to soak up some sun, while others were doing their own thing. As for me, I went back to my tent and laid across my bed. Lunch was missed, so there was nothing to do, but wait for supper. When I awakened, it was time for chow. I really didn't feel hungry, but I went anyway, since you never know when the next meal would be served. Supper was just usual shrimps and rice. It seemed as though that was the only menu the cooks knew, besides beef stroganoff. I picked over my food and found myself heading back towards my tent, when I desired to stop off by the Assistant Chaplain to see how she was doing. I enjoyed being in her company. She was honest, spiritual and genuine, and at the same time naive. I don't mean that in the wrong way, it was just that she trusted everything and everybody, especially the senior Chaplain, who was undermining since the attention was focused on her and not him, I sensed some jealousy there. We chatted for a few moments and then I left to prepare myself for bed. I wrote a few letters and stood in line to take a shower. I despised talking a shower with so many others there; there was absolutely no privacy at all. It seemed everywhere you went, there was someone right next to you. You couldn't enjoy the privacy of reading a book in the latrine without someone entering or invading your space, but I accepted that because there was nothing I could do about it, but it also allows you to think how much we take for granted.

West Side of Saudi Arabia Mountain

Chapter 21

The Wait

The next day was no different than most days; the sun was shining in full beam and formation as it's usual. One good thing happened, we were no longer allowed to wear our helmets and Web belt any more, which should have been abolished long time ago, once the war was over. After chow, I went into my tent to find solitude until mail call. Although I didn't receive any mail, I continued to have hope that someone would be compassionate enough and write to me, so I waited anyway. Mail call was its usual time, about 11 a.m. and I strolled across the sand, only to be amaze that I finally received a post card. It was from my husband, a brief hello and that was it. I am still waiting for my package I had requested since December, but to my surprise, it didn't arrive and every time I talked with my husband, he assured me it was in the mail. So I went back to my tent to reply to my post card, when I heard footsteps at the front entrance tent, it was the Assistant Chaplain telling me I had a Red Cross. At first I questioned her as to what happened? All I could think of is that something terrible had happened to my children. She tried to encourage me and told me I could go to the head quarters to call home. The Red Cross read, "I am sick and in the hospital and in need of my wife to come home", from my husband. It was detailed, but that was the bottom line. I was frantic and panicky as I walked over to the compound to make the call. I had to show military identification before I could enter. There were many phones and computers in the tent, and it seemed very much like the main head quarters. I called home and was unable to get anybody, so I waited a few minutes and tried it again. Then it dawned on me that the time zones was different, so I would have to calculate the time zone and call when I thought someone would be home, so I decided to return at a later time. The Assistant Chaplain and I walked back to the unit and at this time, my mind was going crazy, thinking all kinds of horrible thoughts. She insisted on me staying with her to keep me company, but I insisted that I wanted to be alone. I lay across the bed thinking of what could be going wrong, but I was useless, because the only thing I could think of was disasters, so I decided to listen to some gospel, thinking that would calm me, but I was too upset to concentrate on anything. Thoughts of horror raced my brain, I thought about a car accident or were my children in a car accident, and then I thought maybe my husband had a stroke, since he suffered with high blood pressure. I was restless and helpless, because my family needed me and I was too many miles way to help. I kept thinking what could warrant a Red Cross, since most Red Cross was sent if death occurred or some family member was critically ill. Nothing made this tension any better, but I tried desperately to relax, but nothing was working. I paced back and forth in the tent. I thought about my children, were they in danger, were they evicted? Oh well, it couldn't be finances since I was sending all of my army money home and I had no allotment and besides, my civilian job was paying me as well as using my sick time if needed. Plus my husband was employed and he was making just as much as I was, if not more, so it couldn't be finances, but what if my husband lost his job? Well even if he did, my military pay and regular pay was definitely enough to cover the household expenses, with having some money left over. Oh, it was just crazy thoughts racing through my head, nothing of that sort had happened, I thought. He was just ill and needed pampering or just plain lonely for me, perhaps too many months had past and he was beginning to feel his manhood. "I don't know what's really going on, I'll just call home, maybe I can find out exactly what was going on." I told myself I needed to calm down. I needed to relax because all I was doing was making myself hysterical over something that probably was not life threatening. I headed to the Assistant Chaplain's tent to let her know I was ready to make the phone call again. She pulled something together in a hurry and we headed off to the headquarters. Evening was falling and back home was probably in the afternoon, so I was sure I would get some one home. As we walked across the compound, we chatted, nothing of importance, just idle conversation to make the walk less distance. The weather was calm and there wasn't much breeze, but it was never much breeze anyway, except for when there were sand storms, and then you couldn't enjoy it since the sand made it unbearable by getting into your eyes. We finally reached Headquarters once again, identifying ourselves at the gate. It always seemed so busy there, constant phone ringing and traffic coming in and out. I made my phone call and to my surprise, my daughter answered. She was so excited to hear from me and told me a lot of things were happening and she didn't wanted to disclose any because she didn't want me to be upset. She said that her brothers were fine and Scott had been in the hospital, for his blood pressure. The butterflies in my stomach seemed to calm down now that I knew everything wasn't as bad as I anticipated, but I knew my family needed me from the sound and conversation of my daughter's voice. I told the Assistant Chaplain what was going on and I insisted I must be relieved of my duties to be with my family, who needs me the most; If my husband was ill, he would be unable to care for them properly. She said she would talk to the Chaplain and Commander about it to see if I could go home. I felt so much better, I was able to enjoy chow, but I was still feeling uneasy about my daughter's voice. We have always been extremely close and was able to convey anything to each other, I could not help the feeling the need to be home. The next day, the assistant chaplain approached me and told me I had to go Headquarters to fill out some forms through S1 and have my papers approved by the General. I did as I was told and waited patiently to hear from the General, but several days had passed and I didn't hear a word. Once again, I received another Red Cross from my husband, requesting me to be relieved of my duties, to care for my family. I found myself walking back and forth to the Headquarters regarding my release. During my going back and forth, I later learned that my papers had not been approved by my commander, as I was informed. I was furious and felt betrayed. At that point, I requested to see the General to resolve this problem and speed up my request to be released. I felt helpless and I couldn't believe the system could be so insensitive to my needs. I thought, here I was in a strange country, risking my life for a cause that had no real business of mine, I was doing it was for country. I thought why was I here, was it an issue of liberation for the Kuwait people, or was it a matter of oil and money, but whatever the reason, I was here like so many others, who didn't have a choice because we were American soldiers in the military defending our country and the cause was not imminent. Now my family needed me and they were not allowing me to be released. They were pacifying me and not resolving my concerns. The Company Commander came up to me and said he would look into the matter, being he was a lawyer and had connections, I okay it. He later told me that my husband was in jail for worthless checks. It didn't matter to me if he was in jail or in the hospital, my concern was I had three children home, who were under age and who needed me, and I needed to be there. I could not believe they were inconsiderate of my needs and family concerns. The war was over and there was no need to keep me here, especially when my family needed my support. But then again they probably thought it would cost too much to send a handful of soldiers home and they would be taken care of back home. I became angry and decided to swallow in my own despair, depression. I refused to eat or participate in formation. I sheltered myself around myself. When the next available

Hum-v was headed to town, I was sure to find myself on one. For some reason, getting away from the compound encouraged my sanity and lessened my depression. The town gave me some sort of peace and the opportunity to use the phones. I called home and was able to get my husband, who expressed his concerns about the Red Cross he had sent and not to mention his definition of the military and how desperate he and the children needed me. His voice sounded as though he was angry with me, as if I had control over the matter, and all I was doing there was twiddling my toes, at least he ambushed me that way. I can't express the frustration I felt or the anger I was feeling. I did know my day was not going well and for the first time, I was helpless.

We stayed in town for a couple of hours and then headed back to the compound. We stopped off at our favorite restaurant off the highway to buy some chicken. The chicken there was delicious, but you didn't have the luxury of real American chicken, but it was pretty close. The aroma was inviting, it hit you in the face as you got off the truck; the chicken smelled good and your stomach couldn't wait to devour its nutrients. Headed once again to the compound, the road was full of darkness, as if there were no destination, we couldn't vision vaguely what was ahead of us by the headlights that only seemed to capture a small surface of the road. We had finally reached the compound, but for some reason, it seemed dark and gloomy. For the first time, I notice how isolated the compound was. I felt that we were the only existent, that's how strange and gloomy it looked. I felt sad, reality had set in. I had come to realize how far I was away from home, and I wondered would I ever return. I thought deep within myself as I walked toward my tent, that my Father, who is King and keeper of my soul, was going to get me home sooner than I knew. I could not help thinking about my family, I wanted a big hug and I wanted to know if they were truly okay, but I could only continue to pray, that I soon would be able to return home. As usual, I picked up my tape recorder, put the gospel tape in and relaxed myself from spiritual music. Once formation was over, I searched for the Assistant Chaplain only to continue to resolve the barriers that were blocking me. We headed back to Headquarters, re-issued new forms and waited for an answer. It seemed as though I was pulling teeth, but the journey had just begun. I prayed much that day, because I knew if I did that, my blessings would be answered so I continued to stand on faith. I knew whatever the outcome that it would be okay with me, because there was one man that I trusted and his name was Jesus. So, I went on with my usual function of the day, waiting and anticipating to hear something within the week. I walked over to Linda's tent and chatted with her for a while. I went back to my tent and greeted those who I made contact. Some soldiers were playing games, while others washed clothes and did various other activities, some just lay out in the sun and searched for new identity. Several days had passed and I was waiting to hear the final decision I had been denied. The decision slapped me in the face so hard; I could not help feeling cold and angry. All I could think of was why? The war was over and we were not doing anything that I needed to stay, other than taking inventory of equipment from the tents and milivans that were never opened. I went into deep depression and refused to do anything. There was no formation. I refused to do inventory. I was being rebellious. I refused to eat chow; I would just walk around the tent doing absolutely nothing.

 My right eye began to irritate me and I began rubbing it excessively hard to no relief. Something was in it, but I didn't know what. At times, it seems as it I had conquered the irritant, but it would only come back periodically to haunt me. I tried everything, but nothing seemed to work. I decided to let one of the doctor's look at it, to see if he could rid me of this burden. The doctor flushed my eye with saline, but nothing seemed to work. By this time, my right eye was swollen and red, and the irritant was not as much troublesome as my entire eye was. It was a horrible pain, but I could feel something was stuck to my iris and it was hell trying to locate it. The doctor flushed again several times until he finally combated the problem. It was hard to tell since my eye was badly irritated and puffy. I can not tell you how many times I blinked, but it was twice the amount of time then it's usual. It seemed as though everything seemed to be happening; I was denied release, and my eye was puffy. I couldn't call home, there was nothing for me to do here and I was feeling helpless. I showered early that evening because the only thing that was left for me to do was relax, sleep, and pray that the days would only get better and shorter. I don't remember falling asleep, but I certainly remember being awakened by strange love making noises. The voices were whispered and the bed cots that they slept on thumped, and screech with each motion. As I unfastened my sleeping bag from my head, my eyes followed the noise; it was no other than Sergeant Smart with his mistress. He was a fine soldier, organized and likeable, but I could not understand why he didn't have a conscious. His wife's picture hung directly across his bed as if she was watching over him, but little did she know his mistress had become the center of his heart. They would be together everyday they were inseparable. She would wait at night to visit him, and their bodies would intertwine in one. There was no secret of their love affair; everyone knew it, except his wife. I remembered one night, she visited with only night garments on, as if she was a dog on the prowl or a cheap harlot, lusting and waiting to make her next prey. I felt awful for his wife because she didn't have a clue. I could only imagine how her nights might have been filled with fear and anguish, waiting for her love one to return, but reality was he was never going to be the same. You see, this woman was young and pretty. She had probably possessed the one quality his wife was unable to give him, excitement. The excitement of a new relationship that would eventually fade as time went on, as most relationships do;

and the fact that his wife wasn't there. I quickly stuck my head back under my sleeping bag, rewind my tape and pushed the play button in hopes to block everything I had just witness. After all, this was not unusual, she slept with him almost every night and he wasn't the only one doing it, since most of the tents were co-ed.

Morning came and I dressed as if I was going to attend formation, but I felt ill, so I decided to lie down and rest. I didn't feel I needed to go to sick call, I just felt the need to be left alone. I didn't want to deal with the bureaucracy of the military sick call jargon. I was having intermittent chest pain, nothing I felt warrant sick call, I thought. Besides, I was betrayed, denied, who would care or miss me anyway, I thought. I felt as if I was in prison, trapped, unable to maneuver, as I would have wanted to. I wanted and needed to go home and the army was not releasing me. The chest pain had subsided and I felt much better. I got up and grabbed a cold soda from the cooler and allowed it to quench my thirst. I sat on the bed trying to think of what was I going to do today, until a soldier walked in and I assumed formation was over. The soldier didn't acknowledge the fact I wasn't there and I didn't encourage it. Another soldier came in and said, "Why weren't you in formation," and I quickly replied, "I didn't feel good." He told me there were going to be some Saudi people selling some Saudi items later that afternoon, if I was interested and wanted to accompany him. I decided I would, since I didn't have anything else to do. I diddled around the tent, reading my Bible and thinking through what so far has happened in my life. I didn't feel much growth as an individual, but I certainly had learned to accept and adapt to the circumstances that were out of my control. Maybe I had changed, and didn't realize it. I definitely had become more patient and had the willingness to accept change and to challenge those I was uncertain with. I giggled at myself of my boldness to stand up to the General and Commander; of what I thought was right. I appreciated daydreaming, because it allowed me to focus on my inner thoughts and to bring those hidden ones to surface. Although I was many miles away from home, this land had become my second home. There was some good times that I shared here and there had been times I was in doubt, but my spiritual awareness, always seemed to bring me peace in the midst of the storm. It is ironic that I thought that, because before I left to go to Texas back home, I remember lying in the bed. I was feeling somewhat empty, my marriage was failing and wasn't healthy and my husband had began to drift away, and I received a phone call from a friend, who was feeling much more sadden than I was. She requested for me to pray for her and I did, but after the prayer was over, I began to feel serenity of peace and a song came into my heart that I had never heard before, "My soul is anchored in the Lord." It went something like this: When the storm is raging in my life and although I didn't know it at the time, that my life was going to be interrupted, I had never forgotten that song. There were so much time to reminisce, and so much time for healing. I didn't attend lunch that afternoon; I had a soda, snacked on some crackers with peanut butter, and waited for the time to pass. It was dreadfully hot inside the tent and outside, smothered with humidity. Although they would pull the edges of the tent up to feel cooler, there still was not a breeze. The heat exhausted me as if I had just run a mile, however, I wasn't moving around away. Although some of the soldiers inside the tent would pull the edges of the tent up so that would be able to feel a breeze, there was still no breeze. However, I wasn't moving around anywhere, I still was drenched at times. There was nothing much going on, either out there for the most time; troops filled the chow tent, as if they were not going to get another meal. Some sat and stared as if they saw something we didn't see while the others found their places of solitude, relaxing, writing letters, or washing clothes.

Chapter 22

"Easter"

It was a beautiful day, it was the day that the Lord had risen, the compound seemed peaceful, everyone was in Church or at least it appeared that everyone was in Church. Inside the tent was so crowded, it was impossible to sit, some had to stand throughout the whole service, but it was well worth it. After church some gathered together, talked for a few, while others did other things. We had chow and the lines were long as usual. The chow was good, but it was getting kind of old, the same ole, same ole, shrimp scampi or shrimp and rice. However, it was good. There wasn't a whole lot to do around the compound, just walk around, visit different people in different tents, and make the best of what was available. Luckily, there was a recreational tent that showed movies, but I never seemed interested in those things.

Later that night while I was sleeping, I was awaken about 4 a.m., I was given a sermon, it could have only been from God and the sermon went sort of like, I guess probably because the church was so crowded and it seems that when its Easter or a special occasion, people gather in droves, the scripture was given to me, "what is going to happen to them after Easter". I arose quickly only to write, which I felt at that time was a sermon for my husband, so I wrote and wrote, searched the Bible until I was finished. I was excited about this. God was actually speaking through me, he was allowing me to see things in a different perspective, I was glad. I was so excited, it was hard for me to fall back to sleep, so I decided to stay up to prepare for formation, but I could not wait to call my husband to tell him of the good news. Why is it that the churches are always full when Easter comes? There hasn't been a church yet, that I have been to on Easter that hasn't been over crowded, so crowded that people are unable to find seats. Some end up sitting wherever there is space even if it is on the floor, I guess somewhere deep in people souls, they know there is a Supreme Being, but I know him as Jesus. I was thankful to have a personal Savior, someone I could talk to, someone who could listen without telling, someone I could confide in without having to worry, and not spread my business. It was so good to have a personal relationship with Jesus and his Father. It was awesome how the Bible quotes, how Jesus sits on the right side of our Father and intercedes for us, because God doesn't see us as we see ourselves (in the natural) or as Jesus sees us, (being he was once here in the world in the flesh). I believe God sees us as only as spirits. I was so excited; I could not wait to tell our Assistant Chaplain, she was excited also for me as well. We continued to have church and Bible study and sometimes it was difficult to get the people to come, but we continued to spread the good news. One day while I was in my tent, I decided to go and borrow some books from the tent where we had our Bible books, etc. When I walked in the lights were off, so I didn't notice anything unusual because it was really hard to see, but I heard some noises and when I looked up, it was a Lieutenant and the Chaplain standing, I was in amazement, I couldn't believe what I was seeing. Of course I played it off and acted as if I didn't see anything, but my spirit was sort of dampened by what I believed could have or did take place. I am not saying that anything out of the ordinary took place, but because of the closeness of both of them, it was quite odd that the Chaplain and the lieutenant would be standing in darkness, but nevertheless, so many things was happening here. Perhaps he was comforting her in a word of prayer. Everyone seemed to be down and in despair and maybe he was comforting the dampen spirit, encouraging her to wellness. I was probably more in shock when I heard and saw two females sleeping in the same tent. Rumors had it they were lesbians, and the rumors of the

Colonels and Majors cohabiting with enlisted E-5 and below, did not surprise me neither, too much was happening. Distance somehow made it easier and tempting when men and women are together, they tend to experiment. But despite all the things that were happening, and the chaos that was going on around me, I still continued to keep my faith, and to be strong in the Lord, and faithful to my husband. The good thing about it, souls were still being saved and the mission was not defeated; save souls to get them to Christ, and the Assistant Chaplain and I continued. There are no boundaries in war and sometimes people tend to get crazy or behave in strange ways. It is only natural for the inner self to satisfy their lowest hierarchy, which tends to forget about their self-control. Maybe their lives will return to normal, once they return home at least I hoped it would, for their love ones sake.

Chapter 23

"Are You Ready?"

I was asleep, when I felt a hand tugging at my sleeping blanket, lowly whisper, "Lieutenant Scott, Lieutenant Scott, you were picked to go home tomorrow, be ready at five a.m. in front of the S1 tent". I arose quickly and unzipped my sleeping bag as fast as I could, so I would be able to see who was tugging on me, I was stunned, I was flabbergasted by the good news I had just received. Sleep no longer was important, as I pondered and prepared myself for my departure, I couldn't believe it, I was finally going home, and my name actually had been picked. I was overly anxious, so I did my usual, I prayed to God for his thankfulness and being merciful to me, and I said good-byes. I headed towards the S1 tent as fast as my body would allow me to move. The sky was dark and my bags weighed me down, as I headed towards the S1 tent. I was definitely not alone. There were other anxious soldiers, who were given the verbal instructions that were carried out to the fullest. As we chatted and waited until the person in charge arrived, we were asked to get into a formation as detail instructions were announced. I was bewildered and felt betrayed when my name did not appear on the call roster. I was not going home, at least today. A mix up had occurred and my name along with a few others would be left behind. I slowly excused myself from the excited group with lumps of chocolate that appeared to be in my stomach. The walk back to my tent seemed longer than it usually took, but I really didn't care, because for that moment, everything seemed blank, except home. When I reached my tent, I stopped to look around the compound, which seemed dark and isolated as if it was haunted. Dawn had begun to surface and you could see the sand dust dew on the tents, much visible. I slowly entered my tent, only to find the soldiers getting ready for formation. My peers tried to comfort me, but I was not allowing their encouragement to penetrate the mixed emotions I was feeling. Chow was being served and formation was to follow. However, I had made up my mind; I was not attending, besides, who would miss me anyway. They had denied me the Red Cross request and once again, they were denying me home. It was so much easier to rebel at this time than to attend formation. Unfortunately, the rebellious period didn't last long. A colonel, my chief nurse, ordered me to get my act together and for me to speak with her once I returned back to the United States. I didn't allow her to intimidate me like she always did; however, I expressed my concerns. Besides, how could she speak to me on my behavior, when she was caught herself in an unlawful act against military regulations, not to mention fraternization; how dare she try to reprimand me, my only concern was my children and my husband, she had her lover here and my love ones were many, many, miles away.

The next morning I attended formation, but I was beginning to experience chest pains. Most of the time, I tried to ignore it, but the pressure pain was becoming increasing intense, so I decided to visit sick call. After seeing the doctor, he too suggested I be sent home and ordered to take it easy. Life at that time was easy, how easy did he want me to relax. There wasn't much to do but wait. The doctor recommendation didn't go forth, so I had to endure the pain; however, I did have Atenolol (Tenormin) medication that the other doctor had given me from previous sick call for chest pain, so there was still hope. The days went by very slowly, so I had much time to focus on myself and pre-occupy myself with obligation like writing letters, reading, and visiting my friends throughout the compound and when chance allowed, I visited town. Chow was beginning to bore me. It was beginning to get quite old; it was the same ole menu, day after day, after day. The only thing they prepared was shrimp Creole. I was sure I would turn into a shrimp or a grain of rice. Although I tried faithfully to deny the pains I was feeling in my chest, I remained unchanged, so once again I preoccupied myself with other duties so I would not feel or think of it as much. I was angry about not being allowed to go home, but I knew I should not worry myself about it; after all, I would soon get the opportunity to see my children after and before. Time was winding down and down time seemed forever. My faithfulness to pray continued and that somehow made the anger and wait less. The days seemed as though they wound never end. There was not much to do. I was bored and so isolated as were so many others. I went to mail call to see if I had any mail and to my surprise, I received several post cards and a letter. I was too excited, because it had been such a long time since I felt someone cared about me. I rushed to my tent to read the exciting news from afar, believe it or not; one was from my Sunday school teacher, who sent her encouragement and support. I held those post cards and letters close to my heart, because I wasn't sure when I would be hearing from them again or if I was getting out alive.

Since time had allowed me much space, it was only natural I replied. I fumbled through my belongings, found some stationary and a pen, and did exactly that, wrote them back.

Chapter 24

The Calling, Going Home

Morning would begin with the sky being as blue as the ocean, with puffs of white clouds emerging within them. Formation was never so different, the same ole, same ole, update briefings that really didn't tell you anything, idle rumors, but nothing ever concrete. Not being rude, sometimes I would listen to soldiers to convey their complaints and rumors, but sometimes the information became so repetitive that I listened and allowed nothing to be absorbed. My thoughts were of being united with my family and at that the point, nothing seems to matter any more. I guess I was becoming a bit rebellious; I really didn't want to be here any more. I had done my mission and now I wanted to go home to be with my children. I wanted very much to hold them and kiss them and tell them that everything was going to be all right, but it wasn't happening for me, at least not now. Days had passed and it finally happened, but this time, I wasn't asleep, I was awake. My first thought was when the soldier approached me, was Oh God what now, I thought it was a Red Cross, but it was to inform me I was leaving first thing in the morning. I didn't know at that moment what to think, I was too excited to react, I just sat still, and within moments, I was ahead of packing and assuring that all my belongings were not missed. It had finally hit me, I was going home, and I had to share the good news. I expressed my soon departure news with one of my favorite soldiers, who often sat by the bed side while we heated a small kettle of water for tea, it seemed somehow to relax us while we chatted about the events of the day and home. He would talk for hours about his wife and how he was lucky to have her, not to mention the gifts she had sent him and how he chuckled. You could see the love in his heart. You would think he was a newlywed, but he was grateful and happy for many, many years. His silly coo and his baby teeth smile often would amuse me, as he reminisced about his love. I was not that excited about my love, since he had caused so much strife in my life. He was a liar, a whoremonger, and I wasn't sure if we could ever be happy again. I don't mean to sound careless and cold, but my husband had done many harsh things, that I was skeptical on our happiness. There were just too many hurtful things. Nevertheless, I enjoyed our conversation, because with his love chatter of expressions, there was still hope for me. We continued to chat until we began to yawn one to another and we knew then it was time to retire, but before we did, we said our good-byes and I tuck myself inside my sleeping bag until sleep took control.

The break of dawn came and I found myself once again waiting at S1 to depart; to be set free, but to my surprise, the waiting had just begun. At the formation and a head count, my name was called finally, this time I knew in my heart that I was not going back to stay in the compound, but this time I got the chance to stay. We huddled in little groups of familiar faces, anxiously waiting to go home and chatted about the directions that were given. We walked across the terrain, only to find other soldiers there expecting the same thing, home. After only a few hours of idle conversation and wait, I became thirsty and reached for my canteen to fulfill that mission. Another five-ton had just unloaded unfamiliar faces, but they were U.S. Army soldiers, so we greeted each other with a smile or two. Finally, after several hours, another formation was called, but it really didn't bother me, I was just glad I knew I was going home, but there were times that I thought someone would come from Headquarter with a list saying, I was not. So I battled within myself with the uncertainties from time to time, but I didn't allow the doubt to steal my joy. After several hours of unloading and loading, we were finally ready to depart to our holding facility. The final formation was done and we boarded the buses as they waited patiently to guide us through the terrain to our final site before departure. It seemed as if we would never arrive, but it always seemed that way when you are anxious to get to the place you need to be. For the most of us, some slept and a few of us stared wide eyed as we left the compound of a place we had known to be home away from home, but there was also a sense of sadness because for many there were still friends who had not had this opportunity, we were leaving them behind. I could not help feeling the sadness of what if, but I knew they too would have this opportunity soon. As the bus passed the bumpy terrain, I looked into the sand dust that overshadowed the tent scene, and the tent scene, became smaller and smaller, until I was unable to see them. I then placed my hands over my face and let out a loud sigh of relief and thought the war is over. I allowed myself to think of the good times I had there and of the hard work I had done assisting with the building of the hospital, the long hot days, that had succumbed me and my pigmentation, my nursing and soldiering training that became a necessity, and was well used, the touch of a caring hand, a caring smile and saying encouraging words to the injured, the many prayers sent and answered, and the lives I helped saved. It was all real, it had happened and now my life would never be the same again, I had been there, I had saw, and now I was forced to left go and go beyond what I had experienced, I was going home. I had many thoughts about my arrival, my behavior, and how I would greet my family? I wondered about the change and how much the war had any affected me. Would I experience the post-traumatic stress syndrome, which so many soldiers experience after a devastating crisis? My mind was racing with so many thoughts and uncertainties, and somehow I knew the answers to some of them, but I didn't want the change to be real, because I knew in my heart that I had changed. If the change was small or large enough to be observed, of course I knew I was different. I had just experienced several months of trauma, probably what most people would experience in a lifetime. I could not think of anyone who would want to change places with me. The bus came to a full stop, we were there. It was amazing. When I looked out the window, I saw thousands and thousands of soldiers walking around, I could not believe it, and I would soon be among them. They too were waiting to go home, we had survived the storm and now we were almost to our final destination. I couldn't believe the many soldiers that were there. It seemed as if there was never a war. They were walking joyfully around, chatting, doing almost anything, as if the pressure pot lid had been lifted, and it was awesome to see so many happy faces everywhere. Once everyone was off the buses, we were given our location on which part of the hangers we would occupy. After getting our baggage, we were directed to go inside the hanger and find our places. The hanger inside was large, larger than the one stayed in before we departed to go to Saudi Arabia. Men and women were scattered everywhere. We grounded our gear and headed off to find the showers, which was long awaited. It was unbelievable. The place was indeed swimming with U.S. troops. Once we found the location of the showers stall for females, we also found the shower stalls for the men as well, as they were directly across from each other. Although the lines were long, the wait was not nearly as long, what the others and I was use to. The water felt great, it was exceptionally hotter than what I was use to. I wished I could have stayed in there for hours, but I knew others were awaiting this pleasure treatment and I wasn't going to be selfish. Gathering together, we decided to hunt for food. It was so crowded, it was almost impossible not to brush against someone when you passed them, but they knew it too, and therefore no hostility was ever shown. The food was great. I can't remember all that was served, but one thing, I do remember, it was definitely served hot and the portions were not enough. After enjoying our hot meal, we decided to be curious and found ourselves wandering off to see what the others were doing. There were too many of us there, it was beautiful plentiful faces with smiles and laughter. I believe this was a new era for all of us. We had completed our mission and we were alive to tell our stories and most of all, we were going home. As for me, I was too excited, but deep in my heart, I had mixed emotions. I can not explain my feelings at this time, but for some reason, I wanted to go home, but there was a part of me that wanted to stay. I thought about the proposal to go into Iraq to help the wounded for an additional six months, and why I didn't say yes, but oh well, who was I kidding. I was exhausted: with fatigue, my lungs were filled by black soot, I was tired of sleeping on cots, and the inhaling of the fine sand that tormented me, then I thought, I wanted to be home. I wanted to see my children, who too have suffered the long ordeal of patience and wait, and most of all missing me. As we passed the many soldiers, who seemed elated and full of spontaneous laughter, we decided that the war had been good and not many lives were lost. But we did mourn the lost lives that were not here to share in this finale and prayed for the families who must face the nightmare that their loved ones would not arrive back. We strolled until we found ourselves back to our designated area and found our place of belongings. We decided to rest and wait until midnight when we would depart this part of the world that we have known and learned to discover and explore. My belongings were neatly packed and ready for departure. This was it, I thought, because I knew once I left there, I would never be able to return for some time, maybe perhaps as a reunion, but I knew that would never happen. As I sat there, I could not only think of the children of Saudi and the children of Kuwait, who families were mutilated, they were relieved of their tongues from their mouths their tongues taken out of their mouths because they rebelled against the order they had to fight a war. I felt sadness for this country, sadness for the leader, who had no regard for his people. After the cease-fire, children were at the Evac Hospital where I went for sick call and as we were talking to them, the boy had a bandage covered on top of his head and I said to him, "How are you", and he said, "my sister boom, my mother boom, my father boom, Saddam boom, he killed all of them, he killed them boom." But in reality, I was stunned and in shock, but he talked as if it was a way of life. He showed no kind of compassion. He didn't seem remorseful. I guess if you live in a country like this, you learn to adapt, as we learn how to adapt in our world. To others our culture may be looked upon as different. I could not accept, and can not accept a six-year-old accepting death or the destruction of death, as if it was like sucking on a lollipop and in good standards. It was really a strange place to be, I mean as I look back now and I could see that men ruled this country. Women are not allowed to go out during the day, the only time that they are allowed to go out is during the Ramandan day and that is when they can go to the various market places and shop. Their faces are covered in public places (Khofya veil scarf) and you can only see their eyes. They do not have the freedom to drive, vote, or show their legs, and are segregated from the men. One time when I was in the store, and I was buying some items, when all of a sudden the bells went off and the man just kindly stopped what he was doing, didn't tell me anything and started closing the shop. I mean it was unbelievable; it was like fifty people in the store. They pray a lot, they pray constantly, day and night, when the bell sounds they drop to their knees on their prayer rugs and began to pray. It is really neat, but it is their Muslim belief and custom and I do respect that. While my thoughts went back in time I could visualize them driving, I observed how the men and the little boys sat in the front seat of the car with gas masks and the women sat in the back with no gas mask. I also saw only women and little girls minding the sheep there were no men. Their culture was really strange, but as I said before, it's their culture and we have to respect it. One of my friends, who worked at the hospital in Rdyah, told me how the woman gave birth, she thought it was crazy. It is totally different in how we give birth, when we give birth and progresses to the second stage of labor; we need to be put in a straight jacket from our wild behavior because we are in excruciating pain. They (Saudi women) on the other hand of course, just have their legs in the proper position they are suppose to be in, they do not cry, and maybe the word "ugh", you might hear as they bring the infant into the world. They show no emotion. The father takes the baby and he is very unhappy if the baby is a girl, but if it is a boy child, he is very elated. Of course this country continues with their beliefs, parents still finds husbands for their daughters (better known as arranged marriages) for various sacrificing of certain items, prestige and so forth, but that's their custom. I think one of the amazing things that happened. As I look back and trying to reflect on all the things that had happened was the most terrifying, and of course this happened along with the young child after ceasefire. Saddam had ordered his soldiers to kill off Arabic's children, men and women. A little girl was stabbed in the forehead and she lost her life, but the little boy had survived, and you think how grateful and lucky you really are, but actually we are just blessed people.

 Then there was the time I remembered when we were in town, and I was looking to see females, because that is a Western normalcy, females in our country love to shop, that is just expected; what so many of us do on Saturday mornings. In America when we hear of a sale, of course the right sale, we are clustered in the shopping malls spending our money and trying to catch the bargains. But it was different there. I noticed that there were no women around, they were all men, hugging, walking together, kissing, and this is a normal custom with men. I also noticed men showed no regards for other people. We were all standing in line waiting to use the pay telephone, and there was a man there talking on the phones for five minutes, ten minutes, fifteen minutes, twenty minutes, he looked at us, started digging in his nose and continued talking, as if we weren't there, he looked at us as if he was saying, "I am on the phone now, and you are going to have to wait;" we waited a few minutes before we left, because he refused to get off the phone. In our country, you're proven innocent until you are proven guilty, and in their country, if you are caught stealing, you automatically get your hand chopped off and this is like a big circus event for them. One time I was at the store, and a young man was caught stealing, the alarms and bells went off, and everybody was running downtown to see the show, they did cut his hand off, and of course he would never steal again, at least I am sure he would never think about it. One thing I noticed about them, were when men and women were out together, the men walked ahead of the women and the women sort of lagged behind the man with the child or children at their side. I guess that was kind of strange for me, because I was so use to seeing men and women walking and holding hands together, and stealing a kiss every now and then, although I never seen women there holding hands in any type of way, or showed any emotional bond, but there were plenty of men holding hands, and at some times, they embraced, hugged, and kissed each other as if it was nothing. But I guess that was their custom and they were used to it, it was something that we had to adjust to. Then there was the time one of the soldiers in the tent was so excited about having her first deer meat, it was a popular meat for them besides the lamb, I guess that is why we saw so many sheep. However, chicken, lamb, and deer meat seemed to be their delicacy. Although I didn't have a chance to try the deer meat, I suppose it was good by the way she bragged and had our taste buds savors while she told her story, but I think I would prefer to stick with chicken. As I sat here, I could not help wonder how thankful I was to be a part of a great country, a country that allowed freedom, and freedom of speech, I was indeed grateful. I was awakened out of my sleep with loud noises and harsh voices that requested demands. Apparently, our departure would be delay because an M-16 riffle was missing. As I arose and rubbed my eyes to fully comprehend what was going on, I couldn't believe someone would be that silly to still an M-16 knowing they were on their way home. I guess I was pretty tired because I didn't remember falling asleep. We were told that if the M-16 riffle did not show up, that we were going to have a shake down. A shake down, I thought, what a bummer. A shake down meant exposing all of your gear so it could be inspected. This ordeal was going to happen if the riffle did not surface soon and they meant business. While everyone rose and stood near their belongings, we waited for the final word. After an hour or so, the riffle made its way back to the bathroom where it was confiscated, we were told prior to that no one would be prosecuted if the riffle returned, so at least that option was given, and the case of the missing M-16 riffle was then resolved.

Chapter 25

Home

I wasn't quite sure what time it was, but it was April, in 1991, I do know it was quite early. Our group was informed that we would be departing soon. As we made our way to the front area, we were given a briefing of what to expect and what contraband not to aboard. Understanding this fully, I could not depart from my souvenirs, the sand bottles I had made to distribute to my love ones and friends once I returned home. I didn't know what to do, should I get rid of them or should I tell them, or keep the secret to myself. I didn't know what to do? Because if I got caught with any contraband, I might be prosecuted and my flight would be cancelled. I was caught between a hard rock and hard place, because I wanted so much to keep them, I wanted something so much to remind me of this place. Although I had brought much jewelry and plenty of prayer rugs, and many souvenirs, I still wanted some of their sand. Before passing through the three compartments to depart, there were big poster signs that warned you against taking thing out of the country. "Warning, if you have any contraband rifles, ammunition, this is the time to get rid of it, "all will be prosecuted." Toting my baggage on my back, I continued through, I stood in the line until I was told to come forward to the soldier who would do the final inspection. I quietly leaned half of my body over the counter and said to him in a whisper, when the question arose, "look, I do have two bottles, putting it mildly of sand that I have collected in my possession. His eyes grew wide-eyed as if my being honest was ridiculous and he said, "Where are you going", I said, Florida. He then said to me, "Why on earth would you need sand, don't you have beaches and plenty of sand in Florida." I said, we do, but it is not the same, it is different. The sand is of Saudi's sand and I want to give it to my children as a souvenir." Then he firmly said you sure that is it, and I said yes. Then he said, okay you can go. My heart calmed down and I went through the exit to board the plane. After finding my seat and getting situated, I finally realized I was on the plane, a plane I knew that was destined for home. I waited for my partner to take her seat and we chatted until all were aboard. I guess this was the time reality finally sunk in. I was leaving the desert and some of my friends and I only hoped that they too would follow soon. I closed my eyes and opened them slowly only to assure myself I was not dreaming. I looked outside the window, only to see the blue sky and the few soldiers placing our baggage aboard. Once everybody was aboard, a roll count was called, the door closed shut, and we were ready for take off. As usual prior to take off, we were given a briefing of where to find the exit doors, fire extinguishers, and the oxygen. There were some gossip that there was excess baggage and some of the belongings had to be shipped with the next plane, the very least to worry about, the doors had finally shut close. I didn't think much about baggage, because most of my souvenirs had been shipped home. The engine was reared up and the plane began to move and before we knew it, we were heading down the runway, ready to enter into the sky and return to the United States. I was feeling excited, it was really happening. The day had finally come and a good thing was happening. We were instructed to stay in our seats and keep our seat belts fastened until the overhead signal light came on. As I looked out the window, my eyes discovered a new place, the sky unlimited. My friend next to me voiced words of excitement too. I thanked God silently for allowing my life.

 She said she was ready to see this day finally unfolding. Our eyes mirrored each other and smiles were returned. We didn't have to extend our conversation, our smiles told the story. The take off was quiet as the plane continued to make height. The signal light came on and soldiers started to leave their seats and visit the rest room and their peers. Some even started to watch a video and that seemed like the perfect thing to do. As usual, the stewardesses were very kind, they treated us as if we were super heroes, and they catered to our every need. It was a great feeling to be respected and regarded as special, but I don't think that we should have been regarded as heroes; after all, we had did the very thing our country wanted us to do, free Kuwait and take care of our people and with that main focus our mission was accomplished. Unfortunately, the super heroes are the ones who didn't make it back physically, but those who lost their lives in the battle, to me they are the heroes, and they are everyone's hero. The true heroes are the ones who fought or were assassinated defending our country. I was beginning to feel tired and I needed to rest and I decided to do just that. When I awaken, "Home Alone" was about to start on the screen and this video brought hilarious laughter on the entire plane, except to those who were sleeping; it was just what we needed. The stewardess began to feed us as if we would not see another meal again. It was very similar coming to Saudi Arabia. Our first stop was Belgium, where we refuel the plane, we were not allowed to get off, so we stayed plastered to our seats, although a few soldiers decided to stretch and roam. When the plane was finished getting the fuel it needed, a new group of stewardess came on while our recent ones were saying their good-byes and giving us well wishes. The new stewardess was unique in her own way. They all talked with soft accent and they weren't your regular size 10. I guess things were changing. I believed one looked about fifty years old and a size of a 16, but she was neatly attired and very pleasant. In reality, you don't have to be 5' 8" and weigh 100 pounds to look good; it is the inner beauty within. Once again in the sky, the stewardess greeted us again with open arms; they expressed their compassion to all of us. As we began to travel home, once again we were fed. It seemed so ridiculous to be eating all the time, but I guess they were trying to get our biorhythm together before we returned to the United States. Some of the stewardess walked around and asked many questions, and as always, there was always one question that was always asked, "Were you scared?" These stewardess were much outgoing than the last ones, it seemed that they were pleased by answers. After several hours, we stopped again, not to fuel, but to retire the stewardess who had been so kind. I believe we were in Italy, we didn't stay long, the stewardess exchanged and we were off again. We received new stewardess, who also had beautiful accents, but these ones were the usual stewardesses, you were use to seeing. They too gave us words of welcome and expressed their gratitude in a heart-warming way. Once the plane was in route, the food came again. I was totally stuff and my digestive system was definitely sluggish, so I was unable to eat another thing. After several hours, we stopped again; the trip seemed endless, as if we would never reach our destination. A few naps in between surely helped. I was becoming anxious and restless; I wanted to be home. My partner next to me felt the same way. We exchanged a few words between each other and before we knew it, sleep took over. Once again, we greeted new stewardess as they made their exchange. The accents were becoming less pronounced, and the language was beginning to sound western. I knew we were getting close, but I was not sure how much longer it would take for us to finally reach our destination. The hospitality was extremely welcoming, but after twelve hours on the plane and constant eating, the welcome was wearing thin. I felt if I slept, I would pass the time and hopefully when I awaken, I would be there.

 Within a few hours, we landed again, but this time we were in Maine, and we were allowed to get off for a heart-warming welcome. This was indeed our first welcome home and it was exciting to see and feel compassion of so many people, who didn't even know us. My hat and my heart goes out to all the Vietnam men who served and was not greeted as we were. It was crowded and the compassion of these people was overwhelming. There was so much love in this place and in their hearts, that it was impossible not to feel it. Although I did not know any of these people, they were expressing their concerns and love just by being here and offering their support. They had booths and tables set up with all kinds of paraphernalia, souvenirs, buttons, pencils, papers, pens, and all kinds of gadgets, from literature to addresses. I couldn't wait to call my family and tell them how close I was. The lines for the telephones were not as long as I was use to waiting, so the wait went pretty quick. The first person I called was my husband, but no one seemed to answer. I called my mother, who always seemed to be in place, she was sleeping, but she didn't care, I knew she would be excited to hear from me. I told her where I was and how special this occasion has made me feel. I can not express the warmth I had received and truly color had no barriers. People were hugging, smiling, and chatting with you as if they had known all their lives you before. Yellow bows and ribbons decorated the room with so much love and yes they were everywhere. I was glad to be home, at least almost home. It was just a matter of several more hours, and I would once again be mom. After the hour break and voices of happy good-byes, we boarded the plane and were on our way home again. I believe our last stop was New York. Once again, we were not able to detach ourselves from our seats, but that had become the rule. My friend next to me began to feel nervous, because she knew it was only hours before she would truly be reunited with her love ones. As for myself, I didn't feel nervous, but I didn't know what to expect or say, as I reunite with my family. It was definitely a touch and go situation. I mean, I had so many ideas and what words I was going to say when I met them, but I wasn't sure of what was going to happen. I awakened, only to find myself in Savannah, Georgia. I was getting closer to home, and butterflies began to cloud my stomach.

Prior to departing, we were given a briefing on what to do. My first priority was to find the baggage department and once I found it, they were unable to locate all of my bags, but the claim person reassured me that my bags would arrive soon. I filled out a baggage lost slip and returned it to the claims person. I was disappointed because I believe I still had some souvenirs in the bag that was lost. It was no time to sob over the idea of loosing my bags, even though it was the most important bag; it was the bag that I had the gifts for my children in; I'm talking Saudi symbols and plenty of Saudi's gold, and I believed I had some prayer rugs and dresses in them also. I could not loose them; they were too precious to me. Once we left the baggage department, we were given instructions to meet, so we could take the bus that would charter us back to the mobilization site in Fort Stewart, Georgia. Prior to leaving Savannah airport, I had two missions to fulfill; one was to say a prayer in his honor, and the second one was to kiss the ground to express my love and freedom home. As I boarded the bus, they commuted me safely to my mobilization site; I enjoyed the view that I had so long missed, the green grass, the aroma of the air, and most of all, the civilization of my culture. It was a good feeling to be home. I could then understand the emphasis people place on this country; I knew how one might risk their lives to be a part of this melting pot. After being in a country that standards regarded women as only reproduction machines to breed their children and hopefully they are boys, I could not help being captivated by the sweet waters of America, and what my country represented. I was an American, and it was a good feeling to know my country was special.

On April 22, 1991, I reached my destination, I was greeted by some of the soldiers, I left behind. Although there were not many words exchanged, I somehow knew they were happy to see me. I gathered my belongings to protect them in a safe place until my husband arrived. When I went outside, my husband was standing there with a bouquet of pretty yellow flowers. As I walked over to greet him, our smile exchanged, and we embraced. I wasn't as happy as I thought I would be it was almost as if we were strangers meeting for the first time. I must admit we acted as if we were strangers. This was to happen in fairy tale books, not actual lives, but then again, absence had been distance and I guess it would take some time getting use to each other again. We embraced for a while and he held the bright beautiful yellow flowers towards my chest, "These are for you", he said. I missed you. I told him I've missed him too. We just stood there speechless towards one another, unable to say anything. I didn't have much to say and I thought how foolish of me for not saying more, this is what I had thought of for so long. Maybe our silence towards each other had to do with my looks. I was a few pounds heavier and my black dyed relax hair had turned green and had resorted back to its natural texture somewhat. He did ask if I needed anything and I said, I have two wishes. My first wish was Chinese food and it was if I was pregnant or something, and the other wish was before a can of cold beer. My husband found my second wish far fetch, so he gave me the eye as if what I said was crazy. To my amaze, I thought it was a reasonable request, after all I wasn't asking to do anything harmful, and I just wanted Chinese food and a cold beer. Well, sometimes you get the desires of your heart as long as you keep your faith in the right place, you'll be fine; was my thinking, so my first wish was granted. We stood at a Chinese take out on the base and I ordered a large shrimp fried rice, although I wanted civilization food so bad. I was unable to eat because I had to process in. We returned to my new duty station, a transportation unit; how I was attached to them, I probably will never know. My assumption was I was detached from the unit in Saudi Arabia and reattached to a Combat Support unit out of Germany. Whatever the bureaucracy, I had to be reattached to my unit. Before I processed in, I said goodbye to my husband, since this process would take several days to complete.

I entered the rugged building installation; the lights were dim, so it was fairly dark. A few personnel sat on outdated worn desks chatting, they were curious when I walked in. I signed the logbook and waited until the female personnel could find accommodations for me. She asked if I wanted to have the officer's room that was occupied for almost a week by an enlisted soldier. She said the only thing that was left was the female barracks and if I choose it, I would be the only one in there. At that time, I was tired, exhausted, hungry, and the only thing that mattered at this point, were a shower and a place to lay my head and if at all possible, my second wish a cold beer. I took the female barracks, since it would only be fair to leave the enlisted in the officer room, since she had occupied it for a week. I wasn't probably going to be there long, a day or two, and then I would be leaving. I found my accommodation well suited; a row of bunk beds clustered the room from left to right. There was a choice I had to make as to which bed I wanted to choose, so I decided on the fourth bed on the right. I didn't have any sheets. One thing I did have was peace and quiet and enough space to have complete solitude. And if I wanted to run up and down the barracks I had that choice too. I was too tired to eat, so I secured the door to the room, place my food on the next bed, and fell fast asleep. When I awakened, I was somewhat in a stupor, lost for time, didn't have any clock or watch available, but as I reached down to place my feet on the floor, I discovered a set of sheets, and a cold can of Budweiser. I was so excited that I reached for it, popped the top and drank it down in two gulps. My second wish had been granted and now my heart had been fulfilled. I sort of felt like Cinderella for the moment, I had all of my wishes granted, a gift from God, some may say he doesn't approve of beer drinking, but it was ice cold and very much received. I gathered some of my belongings and headed for the shower. Once again I found myself alone. No one there to bother me. I found the shower stall and immediately turned the water on as the pressure sprayed at me with great force. The water was so soothing, that I found myself standing there doing absolutely nothing. It was a good feeling to be home, all the energy I exerted my brain on what to say or how to act didn't pay off, it was mutual in a sense and I didn't have much to say. I guess I was numb and I knew I needed to learn to adjust. After my shower, I headed back to my palace that awaited me. I was some what rejuvenated, but I still remained tire. I had a few bites to eat, but at this time the food was cold and didn't taste at all appetizing. I covered myself with the sheets and prayed that morning would greet me. It seemed as though morning came early, since my body was use to another time zone, but that didn't stop me from rising early. After a shower and fully dressed, I wondered off to the S1 building to find the plan of my day. I had so much to do and I wanted to do it early, because the quicker I started the faster I would be finished. Home was waiting for me and I didn't want to delay the moment I had often dreamed for. My first thought was the hospital; I had to have a physical before I could be cleared and able to process out. Besides a rash I had developed and a heart that palpitated at times, I was given the go signal and proceeded to my next stop. From the clothing store to finance, to the out processing building where I gave up my active duty green badge and received a go, which completed the out processing phase. I don't remember having lunch that day; I was too excited to get finish, which took nearly all day. I was finished about 3:30 p.m. I called my husband and informed him that I was ready to go home.

 I headed back to the mobilization site, where my belongings were and waited for my husband to return. It didn't take him long, approximately about two hours, before he pulled up. I was there waiting, baggage and all. He stepped out of the car to pack my belongings in the trunk, while I opened the door and went in. As we drove away, I looked back at this once overcrowded environment and I knew then the war was actually over. There was a new era about to begin, I was going home. My home to home was no longer a reality, but an open wound that filled my heart with many memories. It's amazing how fond memories never changes, you may alter or imagine the familiars surroundings, but the memories were as vivid and beautiful as yesterday, although it had been a long time since I passed this way. I was glad to see the wide roads and the variety of color cars, since Saudi people only drove white Mercedes and white Toyota pickup trucks at 100 miles per hour on very narrow streets, and the sand dust over shadowed the neutral color of their cars. There weren't much conversation going on, except my husband talking about things that were happening or what wasn't happening, but nevertheless you always take what he says with a grain of salt, since he had a wide imagination to exaggerate. We were almost home and I began to feel a little nervous, but I took a deep breath, hoping to resolve the feelings I was too familiar with. My husband drove down the Boulevard as he always did, but he turned left instead of right. He explained to me that I had a new house. This was all too new for me and I was too numb to digest the surprise.

He pulled up to a brick house that was bigger than what I had been use to. It was lovely. The lawn was beautifully green and the hedges were trimmed almost perfect. I sat in the car with amazement, because I could not believe this beautiful house were mine. It was indeed a good thing to be home, but more important it was a surprise I didn't expect. As my husband drove the car into the driveway, I received flashes of thoughts inside my head; they were too many to concentrate on any specific one. My husband escorted me out of the car and said with a big smile, "Welcome Home." I climbed a few stairs and held on to the railing as my husband held the door open for my entrance. Once I was inside the house, I noticed my daughter awaiting my entrance. She was as beautiful as the day I had left; only she had grown older. We started towards each other and embraced tightly, that our hugs of dear enchantment became joys of tears. It was a sight to see. We looked at each other with tears of love in our eyes. It had been a long time since we had seen each other that we held each other again as if we would be separated again. I believe this is one of my heart warming memories; there I was standing with my first born child I loved dearly and I was glad to be given the opportunity to hold and see her again. I remembered whispering in her ear, that I love her and told her how much I had missed her. The dog barked and jumped up and down with glee, as I greeted her as well; she still remembered me. I questioned the absence of my boys, who were at school; I longed to see them. My anticipation of seeing them were so great, that I asked to get them out of school early so I could fulfill my long awaited dream. My youngest child was closest, so we decided to get him first, after I had a tour of my foundation (house). I was happy I was home. When my youngest son arrived to the car, his face portrayed a huge smile and my open arms surrounded his small frame. He didn't say much, he was too elated. I then left the school to meet my oldest son, and that would complete my homecoming, although I would have liked to have them all home waiting for me, but this was just as good. It gave me a chance to see the neighborhood and its changes; I had reminisced so long about. The area had not changed much, except there were new stores and constructions of new ones in the making. Arriving at my oldest son's school, I anxiously awaited in the parking lot to see him. I really stood erect when I saw his lean tall frame approaching; he was as handsome as always, and almost as tall as I was. He looked surprised with a silly grin on his face. As I started to walk towards him to meet him, we became closer, and my arms stretched forth to receive him. He had held me tight with silence, but that was nothing unusual for him since he always had the habit of keeping to himself. He was never much of a talker. I asked him questions of how was school and he answered, as always, it's all right. We seated ourselves inside the car, as my husband slowly drove off. I was beginning to feel exhausted as we drove home, but my children insisted we stop to get a bite to eat. I though it would be wise to get my daughter, so she could decide for herself. So much had changed, but the fickle minded making decision of what to eat remained the same; one wanted McDonald's, the other Burger King, and one wanted Krystals, once the decision had been made we settled for chicken. Once home, I had to adjust myself to the unusual surroundings. I was so use to being in the desert, I found myself amaze by the civilian surroundings. I daze myself about visiting every room and visiting the patio, some might say it should not have been hard, because it was home, but for me, I was use to much difference and it felt like a home away from home. I felt somewhat like a stranger, my children were doing their own thing and I felt like I was invading the hemmed stitch, and I was the loose thread. I don't mean to sound like I was being selfish, but the attention I was receiving was limited. Don't misunderstand me, I know my children were happy to see me, but they had their own lives and friends, and somehow I was a stranger trying to re-surface a place in their hearts again. They had missed me for so long, they had adjusted and did well without me. I guess I was being too hasty. I wanted to shower them with questions upon questions, hugs and kisses, and they weren't allowing me to. After a shower, I tried to converse with them, but the communication was limited as well, so I didn't persists, I just found myself in my room unpacking. Weary and tired, I decided to retire for the evening and say goodnight to all. Morning came quite quickly; my usual morning routine was completed. Once seeing my children off to school, I decided to respond and write some letters to people who were kind enough to write me when I was in Desert Storm. Most of them were children and it would only be kind of me to write them back, in which I did and sent some of them little keepsakes of Saudi's sand as a token of my gratitude. It was a wonderful feeling to express my sincere thanks to so many lives that allowed themselves time to thank me. My writing took most of the morning and once I was finished, I accomplished the rest of the morning by unpacking and washing clothes.

During unpacking, I discovered a daily journal I had written while I was in Saudi, so I decided to keep that journal near because I was going to write my experience overseas one day, I thought. My ex-husband came home and told me if I wanted to see my parents, I could see them this week. I thought that was a great idea since I wasn't going to return to work for another two or three weeks, I needed to see my parents, I've missed them so much. I was excited. I started to prepare for the trip, but I was having a hard time finding clothes I could fit. I had gained a tremendous amount of weight and I blamed the Depo Provera injection I received when I was in Saudi (to prevent me from having my menses), they said it would cure the sanitation problem. I ponder around the house feeling fat and isolated, trying to decide what I was going to do. I didn't feel good about myself during that time, but I knew I had to lose weight. I thought for a moment, why was I worrying about what to wear. I had money to buy some underclothes and clothing that would fit, however, little did I know, I was limited on what to purchase. When we arrived at the shopping mall, I felt a little uneasy, it seemed as though people were everywhere, maybe because it had been a long time since I visited the mall. We walked around for a while until I located my favorite store, Lerners. I loved Lerners because their clothing was always beautiful, reasonable and you could get many items for less money. I didn't have any trouble finding what I wanted; every item seemed to catch my eye. I also found a few dresses that would be idea for church, so with the help of my husband's approval, I decided to put them on layaway. Standing in line at the register counter, waiting to be served, a siren went off, and without hesitation and a speedy response, I grabbed my side as if my gas mask was there. The people looked at me as if I was crazy, but they didn't understand, this type of maneuver became my daily task and I had to get use to that I wasn't in Saudi anymore, but in reality, some part of me still was. I chuckled and tried to explain why, but the blank stares did not comprehend or for that matter really understood, especially my husband. After leaving the store, I felt stupid and very humiliated, but most of all, I felt embarrassed. I had so many thoughts and feelings racing through my head, I was uncertain on how I was suppose to feel and how I was suppose to react. Were my actions justified, I thought? Whether I can answer that question or not, I did react and that scared me. I was too embarrassed to go anywhere else; all I wanted to do was to go home and stay there. My husband wasn't very compassionate, he thought it was very amusing, but I didn't find it funny at all. If I could have run home and hid under a rock, I would have. Once home, I proceeded to pack and prepare for the reunion with my parents. My children were home, but they were doing their own thing as usual. Our interaction was once again limited for some reason. I didn't know how to reach them and I didn't know how to try. I did try talking to them, but it was mostly one-question answers and not a whole lot of talk. My daughter did tell me she was having problems at school, but she didn't express in full detail, so I didn't pry until she decided when she wanted to tell me. For some time, they all seemed to say everything was going well in school, so as I always did, I trusted them and took their words. I explained to them I was going to see grandpa and grandma, and they seemed to take it very well and they expressed their permission, as if I was doing the right thing, but they also knew if they didn't wanted me to go, I would stay there with them. I didn't hear anything from the Army, or my fellow troops I guessed they were happy being home, and trying to adjust to home. I did receive a letter inviting my family and I to a homecoming party to welcome us home, but I didn't want to attend. Only because I had gained a tremendous amount of weight and I felt so large and embarrassed, and besides I was going to visit my parents and they were the focus at that time. I needed to see them and they needed to see me as well.

A few days had passed and I was on my way to see my parents, sort of like a mini-vacation for me. It was a long drive, but we had so much fun, we sang, prayed, and talked. The ride was very relaxing, something I needed. I love traveling by car up north, because it gave me the opportunity to visit some of the family in different states that I didn't frequently get to see. We stopped in South Carolina and visited my grandmother on my father's side; we then stopped in North Carolina and visited my husband's family. They were great to visit especially his stepmother. Her favorite dish was pepper steak and she always cooked that when we visit. We didn't stay but a day, but it gave us time to unwind before we continued our drive to New York where my family and his mother resided. Traffic was fairly good; it seemed like smooth sailing. We cruised our way making various stops to refuel and get something to snack on, until we made our way into New York. You can always tell when you are in New York, the dare stares greets you, the garbage, and graffiti invites you, but inside the love of the great city, it was always a great sight to see, as Dorothy puts it, "there is no place like home."

For the first time in a long time, I saw my mother smile; she looked happy and glad to see me. We hugged and kissed as if I was going overseas within the next minute, but it was good and long overdue. I expressed my love for her and told her all about my experience in a short time, at least to a point where she could comprehend. My stepsisters were there and we hugged and kissed as we usually do; they had grown taller and were maturing fast. We settled in for a while and I decided to visit my dad. He was never much for the affectionate stuff, so I initiated the hugs and kisses, but deep down in my heart I knew he was, after all he was one of the few that wrote to me besides my husband, my Sunday school teacher and a few concern citizens.

Afterward, we decided to visit my best friend and her husband, they were elated to see me. I could not begin to tell you the fun and greeting we shared. She was such a beautiful person. We had shared many moments together and had cried many tears. I was honored to have Pam for a friend. Her devout honesty; and her sense of humor was impossible to avoid. Her sense of humor sometimes may me wondered why she didn't excel as a comedienne; she would have produced fond fans. Her bravery was worshiped and I only wished I could have been as strong as she was. Her willingness allowed our friendship to blossom and become closer. When her spirit was up and I was at a low, and vice versa, we were there for each other. We had so much gossip to catch up to and that would require hours. Somehow, we convinced them to return to Florida with us and they agreed. We talked for several hours, had dinner, and talked some more until it was time to go home. It seem like I never had much time as usual when I went home, you want to visit everyone and you can't and those you don't tend to feel disappointed; but you try to do your best. The whole week of the mini-vacation consisted of visiting old friends and hanging out with my parents. Unfortunately, the week was coming to an end and I had to say goodbye, which always seemed the hardest thing to do. Departing from my parents always left me with tears hidden behind my eyes. They always seemed as though they were happy I was independent and wished me safe traveling, but you could always see beneath the plastic smile that they wished I would stay or lived closer. I think within their hearts, they felt I had abandoned them. I often felt sad about their grief, as if the little girl inside of me wanted to stay and please them, but I knew I was a woman and I had a family of my own.

Once on the highway, we stopped several times to get a bite to eat, I enjoyed Pam's company she was funny and full of life. She always knew what to say and her smile radiated a glow. I am not sure if being a full size person had anything to do with her personality and wits, but one thing I did experience was most, full size people had a great sense of humor and knew how to make you laugh. We rode our way into Washington, D.C., only to briefly view the Washington's Monument that stood on the left side as we passed through. After a few hours, we stopped in North Carolina as planned. We were looking for a house. There was something about North Carolina that drew me near. I always wanted to settle there and continue raising my family. My husband and I had big ideas; we were going to pastor over his stepmother's church and have marriage counseling. If anyone who knew us closely knew what we had been through, a very stormy marriage filled with lies, fornication, and adultery, so who would be better equipped than us. We had big dreams to glorify our savior, who we thought had given us the okay. Once in North Carolina, we always managed to stay in Daniel Boone Inn and the reason being, we spent our honeymoon there and it was sort of a sentiment to continue the tradition. So whenever we were in North Carolina, I guarantee you that is where you would find us. We visited his family and visited a few realtors. We went house hunting. I was excited. It seemed as though everything was going in our favor. We went to several houses at different location, until I came upon a big white house that sat on a hill. The realtor was with us, but she was patient in allowing us to make up our own minds. I wasn't really impressed with the inside of the house, but the hill made me decide that I wanted to with that one. My friends were just as excited as we were, but they also allowed us to make our own decision. We went back to the realtor office, filled out numerous paper work and was asked to send back a $1000 earnest fee. Of course I thought that wasn't hard to do since I had more than that. I didn't spend any of my military money, so I agreed to her terms and we shook hands to bind the deal. As we drove off, I wanted to see the house one last time, before I left North Carolina. However, my husband made a wrong turn and we were lost. As we were driving, we came upon a house, sort of isolated from the road, sitting alone in the country, surrounded by lots of tall trees. My eyes lit up with astonishment, and I said, this is the house God has for me. I quickly stepped out of the car and walked quickly to the front door. I patted the front door with the palms of my hands, as if the door was made of gold. I whispered words of spiritual prayers to bind the house up; a symbol of words as to say the house belongs to us. Unfortunately, the door was lock and we were not able to enter, so my husband and my girlfriend's husband went to call the realtor. We walked around the house, and were able to glance inside the house through the windows. I thought this was definitely the house I wanted, secluded from the city plenty of trees and much land. The house had a double garage, a deck, and a hammock. I knew this house was the house, because out of all the houses I had seen I felt an emotional fulfillment that I didn't feel with the others. Once they return with the keys, we were able to see the inside of the house. The inside was just as beautiful as the outside. Once you entered a small foyer, a staircase welcomed you. On the right hand side was the living room, equipped with a fireplace, and a bar deck dividing the living room from the kitchen. The upstairs master bedroom was large, extremely, with a huge bathroom that had a Jacuzzi in it, I thought I could live with that. On the opposite side of the master's bedroom was a medium side room that I had already claimed as my son's room. Downstairs was also a bedroom, which I said that I would let my daughter have. There were two bathrooms downstairs as well and two bathrooms upstairs. I could not tell you how happy I was at that moment. The kitchen was beautiful too; it was large enough to put everything you could imagine in it. I had so many ideas on how I would decorate. Our decision had been made; we had already changed our minds about the other house, and decided on this one. We returned to the realtor and expressed our decision. She thought we had made a wise choice, although she stated this house was slightly higher than the other was, as far as cost went. All I could think of was to hurry home so I could send her the earnest fee to bind the contract. My husband also had felt the same way, but he was quieter than usual as if he knew something I didn't know. Whatever his silence represented, all I wanted to do was to get home and send the money back. Before leaving North Carolina, we said a prayer and headed towards the highway.

After a few hours of driving we decided to rest, we were in South Carolina, South of the Border. We sat there, played some games, and again headed towards home. Not much conversation was surfacing, by this time, everyone was sleepy and tired, although we were getting closer, it seemed as though the closer we got, the farther we seem, but that normally is the case when you want to get home in a hurry.

The next thing I knew, we were in Florida. I had just glanced at the welcome sign before approaching the welcome rest station. There wasn't much traffic I can recall, so we decided to stop to use the restrooms. Between my husband and I, we gave them a verbal tour as we entered our county. I can tell they were impressed by the smiles on their faces and their silent conversation other than coos and ahs. I believe she was excited, not so much of the beauty of Orange Park, but because she could not see graffiti or garbage overtaken the neighborhood. It was good to be back home, but most of all; it was good to have my friends along with us to share in our happiness.

Chapter 26

"The Disaster"

The house was quiet when we entered and the children were at school. It didn't take my friends long to make themselves at home either. You see, we were a family; we had so much in common. Pam prowls the house as she guided herself a tour. She said she was glad something good had come out of all I had been through with my husband. What she really meant was, my relationship with my husband had finally reshaped itself and he was finally being a husband and taking care of his responsibilities, she thought. Although I wanted to comment on her praise, I felt it was best to leave things as they were. My husband had appeared quite different, and he had made some changes, I thought, but then again, I had experienced so many set backs before, but I was willing to let bygones be bygones and enjoy the good times while they were remembered. We didn't have much to do that afternoon, other than watched television, chat for a while, and chuckled with laughter about the good old times. We reflected back to the times when we were in the world (not living a Christian life), and how Pam and I would drank alcohol spirits, dance and play old records, while we acted silly. We laughed about those times, how we would stay up plenty of nights having a good time, until the Lord called us home.

My husband and our friend went to pick up Garland and Lakisha from school. My oldest son had the privilege of riding the school bus. Everyone arrived back safely and we all did our own thing. This was my daughter's last year in school, so she confined herself in her room to study while Joseph and Garland played with their friends until their curfew. The night went sort of fast. Pam and I prepared dinner and after dinner, we all headed in different directions to retire for the night. It was such a good feeling to be home, but some how I felt I didn't really belong there. I enjoyed being with my family, but I guess they weren't ready for me or they had adjusted so well without me, that they didn't know how to accept me. The morning was as usual, the children headed off to school, and Pam and I chatted like we use to. She had wanted to go shopping at the mall, so we decided to put that on our list of things to do today. My husband slept during the day, since he worked at night, so this was his time to get some rest. Pam and I went to a few stores and purchased a few items. It wasn't like we had plenty of money, since my husband had my bankcard and I was limited with cash. We had a good time, sight seeing, but probably would have had a better time if we had more money, but nevertheless, we made the best out of the situation and enjoyed wishing and hoping.

Once we arrived home, everyone was there, except my oldest daughter. While we were sitting around in the living room chatting and my husband's friend were attending to washing dishes, when all of a sudden he said, the water stopped. This episode would be the beginning of a long process, I wasn't sure of and a new beginning for me to take a closer look in the mirror of myself. We had noticed a man passing by the window, but we didn't know who he was and what his intentions were. He had come to disconnect my water and I was placed in an embarrassing situation in front of my friends. Although we were like family and I was sure they would understand, but I just felt that it was an embarrassing situation to be in. My husband jumped up and said he would take care of it, and as always in a crisis, he somehow managed to come through. In a couple of hours, our water was turned back on. In privacy, I asked my husband what was going on and he replied, nothing, I have taken care of the matter. I was disappointed because there was no reason for this to happen. The army sent my entire money home regularly and my husband also received pay from my other job, plus his own salary. I didn't dwell on it as much, but I knew deep in myself, something wasn't right. When things were much quieter, I also asked my husband about the earnest fee, the thousand dollars that was suppose to be sent to the realtor as soon as we returned home. He mumbled a few words and never gave me a concrete answer. I was trying very hard to be patient, but I really wanted this house and didn't want anything to jeopardize. Returning to my friends, her facial expression was in awe. She tried to be tactful in words, but she knew as well, something wasn't right. After a few days, our friends were ready to depart and of course, my husband had offered to return them to New York as a way of saying thanks for coming. I wasn't going, besides this gave me the weekend to be with my children alone. It probably also gave my husband a chance to be with his mistress, (who lived in New York) but at that time, I didn't know that. The day had come when we would again say our good-byes; we hugged, kissed, and they left. I was indeed a new beginning, I would finally get a chance to know my children again and this would definitely complete one of my homecomings. My children and I sat around the living room and talked for a while that afternoon. I learned everything wasn't as well as the family had portrayed. Lakisha was having a hard time in school, trying to complete all her prerequisites and requirements she needed to graduate and my younger son had missed a total of thirty-eight days in one semester and was going to be retained. Finally, I was made aware of what was going on. The skeletons in the closets were surfacing, whether I wanted to believe it or not. I was glad they felt honored to confide in me, after all this was the family I once knew. We had always been so close and it was a pity we were acting like strangers and had to learn each other all over again. I could accept that it was going to be like this for a while, that their behavior was going to be like this as well since I was gone for a while. That didn't change the fact that my main focus was how I was going to resolve this situation and what I could do to make it better. I could not believe my husband allowed our son to miss so many days at school. I knew all what they were telling me was true, they weren't children who would lie. They also expressed concerns about the monies and how my husband was renting Lincoln Continental cars every weekend and acting like a big spender. I can certainly relate to what they were saying. You see, my husband likes to be flamboyant, even if it meant at your expense. He loved showing off and having people believe he had more than he had. I had been so long manipulated that I wasn't able to show my anger in which I had all right to be, but I had my Savior, my Father who would guide me through this. I wanted to fix things and make it better for my children, but I didn't know if I would be able to pull it off, since it was very close to the deadline and time was essence. My first thought was to go to the schools and get to the bottom of this. The school system was liable for these mishaps as well, I thought. How could they have closed their eyes to the neglect, regardless of whom was at fault, I had to do something and a hell a lot of singing to resolve it. Garland school was helpful, but the only thing left to do was to retain him, so we both decided on summer school. It was hard to express this to my son that his summer would be obligated to school studies and he would have very little of play, but it was for his better interest. He was awfully shy and his reaction was, why? How could you explain to a little boy of tender age, that he was being held back because of an adult negligence. It seemed always easy to displace the unwanted behavior on something else and stand up and face the music, but I loved my husband and I was used to making whatever he did sound better. In so many ways, I didn't want my son to know how dysfunctional his father really was and I didn't want him to think he wasn't love. However, I wasn't going to camouflage his behavior any more. I simply told my son the truth, but as usual, I always found room in my heart to sugar coat the tongue of words. I am not sure if he really understood, but one thing he did understand, that he would be attending summer school at another school, which placed difficulties since there was no bus route in our neighborhood. As for my daughter, she was in the same predicament; she had to make up a class she didn't know she needed, and she would not be able to participate in the initial ceremony. She was devastated and hurt. She had worked so hard to enjoy the one day she would not be able to attend. Although she acted as if it was okay, you could sense that bothered her. Having resolved the issues that needed proper attention, my next step was to speak to my husband. He always had excuses and always found ways to turn the situation at hand around to precipitate sympathy. He didn't express much compassionate at all; he just gave me a sob story that he was ill and that was the reason Garland had missed so many days. I listened to what he was saying, but I was no where convinced. Our relationship started to turn sour. He was becoming isolated than usual and stayed away from home. He always had something to do that needed his individual attention. He thought himself to be important and that meant frequent Church meetings, guest speaking that sometimes took him away afar. Recently, leaving New York, he was invited to speak at a church, that he was friendly with the Pastor. It didn't matter to him whether the bills had to be paid or not, he had this mission to do and that was how he was.

We talked to each other about our relationship and our situation; he bluntly gave me an ultimation to give him my entire paycheck or divorce. He tried to be convincing on how my paycheck would be spent, but I wasn't buying that garbage; I knew of him too much to take a chance giving him my entire paycheck. My thought was either we did it together or we don't do it at all. He was hostile about my negativity, but I had to do what I thought was best for my children and me. I must admit I felt awkward and guilty about my stand, but I knew in my heart, it was the best thing to do. He quietly gathered his belongings and stormed out the house. His control and manipulation wasn't as effective as it was in the past. I had over the years felt myself finding ways to make it better, but this time, I wasn't going to allow his temper tantrum to penetrate me. I was going to make it better, but for my children and myself. Feeling guilty, my decision stood firm. I plundered around the house, finding things to do, re-arranging this and that, that needed no changing until I decided to get ready for work tomorrow. I would be returning to work, so I needed to find clothes I could fit. I was excited about my returning to work. After all, work and being a mother is pretty much what I had grown accustomed to. I guess I was the only one excited about returning to work, my kids could probably have cared less, at least they showed no euphoric emotions.

Chapter 27

Departing Intimacy

I wasn't too happy when I first arrived at work because I was assigned to another unit without being asked; nevertheless, I adjusted. I did receive a big welcome back from my co-workers, which made the night bearable. Work was exciting, especially on my new unit. The patient's were much sicker and the high level of stress was definitely more. My real love was on the other unit (SRT), my favorite. I missed my favorite co-worker that worked on my old unit; he always had a good sense of humor even when the night was very stressful. Although I knew some of the people on my new staff, except for one female I didn't know. Probably it was best, since her life seem chaotic; she was persistent in trying to make my life just as uncomfortable. I was expected many questions about my journey to Saudi, but it seemed people were walking on eggshells, being cautious of what to say. I am not sure if they were prompted before or not. I stayed after work for a while, chatting with my favorite co-worker. We had so much talk to catch up on, but a few minutes after work would not allow us to, so we opted to gossip later at work.

The drive was longer than usual, probably because I was tired and wanted to get home, not knowing another war was waiting there too. Once I arrived home, my husband, who has no qualms about his hostile behavior, greeted me. It was all too real, he wanted to talk about our marriage and all I wanted to do was to shower and get some sleep. I was becoming more independent and he was loosing control. His way of loving was controlling, by dictating the way I should be, the way I should act, and how I should spend my money. To this day, I resent any man who tells me how I should spend my money; if they want to get along with me, don't tell me how to spend my hard working money. God is working with me in that area and I'm praying on that area as well. While he pouted about the house and showed his two-year-old tantrums and after voicing his thoughts, I showered and tucked myself under the covers. I'm not quite sure what time it was when I awakened, but the house was still. It wasn't long though, until one of my children arrived. I sat on the side of the bed and prayed to my Father that he give me strength through this ordeal. Once again, I had to often call on Him when I was in trouble, that sometimes, I could imagine him saying, "Loretta, give me a break", but I knew in my heart, he did listen and always he seemed to come through just when I thought he had forgotten about me. I was tired mentally, my marriage had begun to fail and I couldn't understand why I had to suffer the burden, but I knew it was for the good, even though I felt weighed and smothered.

I bounced myself up and walked into the kitchen where I found my son drinking his usual drink kool-aide. I didn't know what kind of dinner I was going to prepare that evening, but I did know it would be something simple, since I had to work. I asked my son, how was school, while he did his homework at the table. It was close to time to pick up my oldest, so I quickly dressed and did exactly that. By the time I stopped at the market, it was time to pick up my son. I always felt good having my children around, they are spoiled rotten, as one would say. But if they were, it was only because I spoiled them, and they was a genetic piece of me and that's what made me happy the most. It didn't take them long to adjust to noisy behavior, if it didn't happen, they wouldn't be my children. When we returned home, guess who was waiting, my husband of course. He always looked so pitiful when he couldn't get his way, but this time, I was standing firm on whatever I said. He wanted to talk to me about our relationship. Our conversation wasn't much of anything than usual. All the blame focused on me; why it was my fault and why things weren't the way they were. Yes, I thought it was my fault; I didn't put my feet down any sooner. I gave him the benefit of the doubt and allowed him to speak. As usual, he had to go out of town to speak, as usual, I wasn't invited. When I showed off my special temper tantrum and needed additional attention, I was labeled disrespectful and was not behaving like a wife should. It was useless trying to convince someone who really didn't want to be here to stay. Maybe I didn't have the energy I thought I had; maybe I wasn't as strong as my mother said I was. One thing I did know I was mentally tired and plain drained. I couldn't help feeling isolated and abandon once again. At one point, I reasoned with myself, why I wanted my marriage to work, but on the other hand, I didn't know I had the energy to sustain the entire shortcoming. My children always seemed to sense when I was down. It seemed as though they would become more loving and cooperative without questioning. One thing I didn't need during this time, were disobedient children. In their own special way, they tried to console me, especially my daughter, she always said, don't worry mommy, "everything will be fine." I knew deep in my heart the situation just wouldn't work out. There were too many things going on and this one seemed almost impossible. I tried very hard not to indulge myself into a pity party, feeling sorry for myself, but I couldn't help feeling desperate inside. I felt as if I was the only one in the world and trust me, that is not a good thing. One thing I knew for sure, that always seemed to help, was prayer. It seemed as though when I prayed, I felt better, as if the burden was being lifted and I felt light afterward. I lay across my bed, hoping to get some rest until I rested my very mind, but the thoughts of my marriage kept eating at me, as if I was to blame. In some way, I was partially at fault, and I was trying to fix things and trying to make it better, but in reality; I was making it worse. I could not allow my subconscious to win. When I awakened, I had an hour to get ready for work. I didn't realize how tire my body was until I laid down, it always seemed as if we could go forever, until our bodies are laid to rest and sleep overtakes you. Work was always exciting; you see I worked in a mental facility where we treated individuals with all sorts of emotional handicaps, from homeless to schizophrenic, psychotic, and to suicidal attempts. There was always something going on and some nights I could admit as many as ten patients. The job wasn't easy, but with patience and a love for on hand nursing it was worth it. My staff was dealing with all kinds of personalities, some of them having more than two or three of them. The night usually went fast because there were so many situations going on.

When I arrived home, the house was still, as if no one lived here, even the dog didn't greet me anymore, and she was too busy finding mate as usual, no matter how I tried to keep her tame, she was in heat. My routine was its usual, work, home, and children; this went on for a few days. My husband return one morning without hesitation He didn't rave about his trip, as he often did, he was extremely quiet. I carried on as if he wasn't there. Later that week, we were at the table again trying to find resolution to our problem. During our conversation, he talked about me having another child, as we had briefly discussed when I called home from Saudi, after I happily announced I was thinking about writing a book. Once I confirmed that a child right now would place additional strain on our marriage that was nowhere solid, he stormed out of the room like a two-year-old and called me untruthful loudly. I wasn't insulted personally, because I knew this was one of his tactics to get his way, but nothing on this earth could or would change my mind. We had really begun to drift apart. We were silent to each and later didn't speak at all. This pattern went on for weeks. It was killing me inside because I didn't know what to do or how to resolve the problem. I was totally hopeless. It had gotten so bad that we slept in the same bed without saying boo to each other. Some nights, he would change position and sleep opposite of me. It was all too real, we were departing intimacy and as a couple so close, was now a couple so grown, and so far apart. Although the silent treatment disturbed me, I somehow, with my Father in heaven, was able to overcome it, but there were times when I was weakened. Our children noticed it also, so they tried to do and say kind words to make it easier for me. I prayed often. It was the only comfort outlet I could do without being criticized or questioned. Our relationship began to take its toll.

One morning, while I was getting ready for church, my husband asked me are you going to our church, and I told him no, I told him I was going to visit another friend's church. He gave me an angry look and stormed out of the house and went into the driveway, he popped the hood to the car and did something to the car and I'm still not sure exactly what he did, but I believed he took a wire loose, so the car wouldn't start. When I went outside, the car did exactly that, nothing. I was furious, because he was already torturing me mentally, but this time he had gone too far. I raced to the kitchen-, and I remembered my children and nephew sitting patiently waiting for me to get dress. The next thing I knew, two policemen were at the door, instructing me what would happen if they had to make a trip out here again. I remembered my husband telling them, she just returned from overseas, and she has post-traumatic stress syndrome. I thought how cleaver he was; he had learned a new word and was trying to put it in full use, by suggesting that I was mentally unstable. Maybe I was mentally disturbed since I allowed myself to be manipulated many years by such an insensitive human being who was supposed to be my husband. Or maybe I was dedicated in my marriage besides having the love of Christ. My children were talking to my mom and all I could remember her saying was, stay calm, don't admit to anything and my sister echoing in the background saying, "don't worry, I will be there soon." I continued to get dress for church and called the Pastor and she came to get us. The Pastor was like my second mother. I depended on her for spiritual guidance and strength and she had no problem fulfilling the commitment. The children sat there quiet and in near shock. They were emotionally upset and I didn't have a clue on how to calm them, except the usual sayings, everything would be all-right. Church was uplifting and we went out to eat afterwards as we normally did prior to evening service. When I arrived home, I noticed the cars were gone, except for one. When we entered the house, items were in disarray. I quickly walked through each room, noticing things that were disorganized and missing; the televisions, VCRs, and telephones. I grabbed my head as if I did not believe what I was seeing, but it was true, my husband had moved out, taking as much things as he could some which belonged to him and then some. I couldn't think straight, my mind was racing a mile a minute, too fast for me to concentrate and sit down think rational. My only thought was how could he do this to us, especially me? All I ever try to do was help him, not hurt him, why was he hurting me so badly? My children and nephew were also in awe, they couldn't believe it either, but it was true. His clothing was gone and there was very little left that could remind us of him, just a few pictures that hung on the walls. I sat down, I wanted to cry, but the tears refused to come. I was somewhat baffled, but I wasn't as shock as I thought I would have been. After all, I was given visions prior to in my dreams that this day would come. Although the dreams were strange, they were beginning to happen. As I remembered correctly, one dream actually told me, my husband was leaving. He was standing in an empty house and when I arrived he said, "Loretta, we've been robbed," just as the voice told me he was leaving. Somehow, I was being prepared, so the hurt was not as great. As I sat there thinking, I remembered one dream showing me soulish ties. My husband and this unfamiliar lady were dressed in the same clothing, when I asked, who is this woman, I was told she was a woman in church, who had just received a new position. Later, I discovered that the woman was a friend of ours, and her father was a preacher in New York, that would explain the long distance trips. Whether you believe in God or in some Supreme Being I believed God was preparing me so that the hurt would not be so great. I sat there for a while trying to regain my composure. I somehow regained my thoughts and allowed what had just happened to be bygones. I wanted to forget about the emotions, I was feeling my family had been abandoned and I felt like a failure and isolated. Although I tried hard to deny what was happening, but I couldn't hide the fact that I was alone faraway in this state with no family. I called my spiritual sister to tell her what had taken place; she was comforting and gave me spiritual guidance. I wanted to call my mother, but I was afraid and more than often reminded of "I told you so." Maybe that is what I needed to hear, since I was too hard headed to recognize it sooner, but I really didn't want to hear that. What I wanted was empathy, so I called the people that would give it to me. Although they were of great consolation, I needed my family the most. I needed to belong, so I decided to call home. My mother surprised me, although she talked about everything in the world, but she did console me, and informed me my sister was coming later this week.

 I appreciated it being a Sunday, and church service was good because I don't think I could have made it through another day. I gathered all that I could and rearranged the disarray items that were left behind. To this day, I am still looking for things that we're missing. I finally found myself along in my room. I showered and laid across the bed looking into the ceiling. My thoughts were trying to resolve what had happened, until sleep took control.

 Morning arrived as its usual, the children waiting impatiently while I quickly gathered on some clothing to take them to school. Driving them to school, and now as a single mom, reminded me of what to come and it wasn't going to be easy. However, in a way, I had been a single mom all along. I began to feel dreadfully lonely. I was in my mid-thirties, I was alone in a State that I was not familiar or comfortable with; I was too outspoken. I knew I would be able to survive, after all I had survived the Desert Storm with less resources and here I was in a state that had many resources, how could I fail. But I had failed; I had failed at another marriage. I didn't know how to begin my life again. I didn't know what to do first. I was so use to playing the role of a wife and mother and with a blink of an eye, my role had suddenly changed and I wasn't sure how to begin again. You see, I had been so use to thinking in a two-role capacity, that somehow, I got buried. There was so much to do and so much to adventure. I was literally single and I didn't know how to start again. I dropped my children off to their schools, while I driving back home, I decided to stop at the bakery and buy me a pastry; after all I was fulfilling the void, why not.

When I arrived home, the house was empty and the dog wagged and looked confused. Finally, separation thoughts hit me and reality had set in. My husband had left me, and that is all I could think of. I began to cry and tears rolled down my face as fast as my eyes could excrete them. I ran to my room and grabbed my Bible; I always found comfort when I went to my Father in heaven. He was genuine and I knew I would receive spiritual strength. I could trust Him and I didn't have to worry about Him ever leaving me. I weep until I could not weep anymore and found myself balled up in a fetal position across my bed holding the Bible firmly as if it would walk away if I closed my eyes to sleep.

After I picked up my children from school, we tried to decide on dinner. We usually found it difficult to decide, since everyone had their own desires, but the decision was always finalized and always depended on how much money was available. I didn't feel like eating, so I retired early than usual, so I would not be tired later at work. My sister was coming down sometime this week and I was elated. Her furniture would meet her here, so I had something to look forward to. A few days had passed and her furniture arrived as planned. After the movers unloaded all of her furniture into the garage, their jobs were completed, and I was exhausted just looking at the amount of things she had. I wondered how on earth she had accumulated so much. Nothing had changed. My husband remained exiled, except for leaving the harassing letters and religious pamphlets he left title, "What God Really Expects a Home to Be". Unfortunately, he has never read it or he would have taken his own advice. I needed my sister more than ever now, I felt so alone and frustrated. Why didn't he leave us alone, he didn't care about us, I thought, because if he did, he would not have left us? I knew his leaving was another woman, because he would always act strange or leave us when he met someone new. Why was I torturing myself I thought, but reality is the truth. I can't even count how many times he walked away and as always, there was always a woman in waiting. I was beginning to get weary, because deep in my heart, I knew this was the last goodbye and he wasn't coming back. My mind was too clouded to think about the future, because a part of me continued to love him and a part of me wanted to be hurt free and free of him.

I talked to my family, and learned my sister had a delay; she was not arriving as planned. Great news, I suppose, maybe it was a chance for me to regain some composure before she arrive. Of course, I didn't want her to see me as a basket case, but I felt I had let her down; I had failed at another marriage. A few weeks had passed and I had lost a significant amount of weight and was looking more like a basket case. My self-esteem was shattered I didn't care about my appearance, as long as I went to work, played my role as a mother and paid the bills, I was satisfied.

One evening, I called my best friend when I was feeling low and depressed and didn't know what to do. She would comfort me and give me words of encouragement, even when times weren't kind to her; I will never forget her. We talked about anything and everything, and she always made an effort to point out to me the good things I had done to strengthen my marriage. She was a heart warmer, and kind. Her voice was graceful and enlightened, but firm. She always managed to stay positive. When I talked to her, I always felt uplifted. We would sometimes talk for an hour or more, but we respected the economy of the financial strain and tried very hard to keep our conversation to a minimum, sometimes that meant, a brief hello and a how are you. I welcome her strength and looked to her as a positive role model. I was still receiving those sympathy letters from my husband. He at times had me so confused. One minute he was saying he needed space and wasn't going anywhere, while on the other hand, he was saying, he wanted a divorce. However, his actions on not supporting the family, spoke so much clearer. It seemed as though everything chaotic was happening to me, the car was beginning to give me trouble and a simple tune up for a Mercedes was more than my pocket book could afford. Although I was in this turmoil, I desperately struggled to continue with life. There were numerous times when I felt I couldn't do it, but with God's grace or some Supreme Being, if you want to call him that gave me inner strength. My strength from Christ and my children were all that kept me alive and motivated. It wasn't easy, sometimes I felt as if I was the only one going through, but my God reminded me with His comforter daily, I wasn't alone. There were so much things happening in my life. There was a rumor that the bombs Saddam used in Saudi Arabia were full of chemical agents, that is just what I needed to hear, so when I verified the rumor with the unit. I was told it was all a rumor, and not to worry. There was much to do about what was happening, but everything was as usual no one knew exactly what was really happening and the truth was farthest away, so the problem of speculation remained a mystery.

    I continued to find strength and peace with my Father in heaven. The letters had become scarce and now I began meeting my husband at a nearby restaurant, now I chuckled to a naiveness I portrayed, and just how silly I was to be so vulnerable. Those meetings weren't easy, they were dreadfully hard. I would get home from work about nine and rest for a few hours and meet with him about 1 o'clock. The meetings were useless, but I continued to subject myself to be ridiculed, with harsh words and manipulative behavior. I didn't know then what I was looking or hoping for, I didn't really think hard about it, why I did it because those meetings were not meaningful. Maybe somewhere in my heart I was hoping for him to say, let's get back together, but after these last few meetings, I could feel the distance between us. The love we had for each other was buried with too much animosity and hurt. I look back now, and can say, he might have been jealous of me; my ambition and my willingness to venture on new awareness. Then one day, I was to meet with him again, not knowing this would be our last time being civil towards each other. I was running late that afternoon, because the car was giving me problems, only accelerating at 20-30 miles per hour on a 45 miles per hour zone. It took me forever to get there. When I arrived, his facial expression looked upset, as if he wanted to say, what took you so long. I quickly tried to pacify the situation, so our meeting would run smoothly. I explained to him the performance of the car, the excuse while I was running late. He didn't appear too satisfied, but nevertheless, I wasn't going to be disappointed.

We exchanged brief conversation with one or two word sentences in regards to;" how is the family", "they are fine", etc. A few blank stares when our eyes met, in which a silence was between us. I began to pray "My father in heaven give the right words to say," I wanted to keep peace. As he pondered on with concerns that were not directly towards reconciliation, I interrupted after a mini-voice told me **no more**? I then excused myself from the table; quickly saying I wanted to use the restroom. When I approached the restroom door, I pushed it open, only to find solitude and to catch my breath. I was the only one in there so I began to pray to my Father, that he would give me kind words to say, but my father was greater than I and the voice being of the **Holy Spirit**, said, "**NO MORE.**" When I returned to the table, he continued to ramble off, interrupting him for the second time, I said to him, this would be the last time I would meet with you. His eyes widened in amazement, I guess he didn't quite get it, so I repeated myself again and said goodbye. As I left the restaurant, I didn't know what I was feeling; one side of me felt joy, but on the other hand, there was much sadness. As I slowly drove off, I turned my head only to see him standing there with his mouth wide opened in disbelief. The car was going so slowly, it seemed as if I was never going to reach home. When I reached home, I was relieved I thought I would not allow myself to be humiliated anymore. I was ready for a divorce; it could not have come sooner. One day while I was at the laundry mat, I ran into one of the workers who knew my husband and me. He chattered some words my husband had told him, and I politely told him, the only thing my husband could do for me was give me a divorce. Within several weeks, I received the divorce papers, my husband had filed.

Chapter 28

"It's Over"

Once received the divorce papers, I too sought a lawyer and was informed to countersue. If I knew the outcome in head of time, I don't think I would have gone through it. The process was awfully dreadful hard work. I had to do a lot of footwork to decrease my expenses, that I somehow felt I was a lawyer. I visited the courthouse, pawnshops, utility companies, and received many print outs and affidavits. I had so many copies and statements; I knew my lawyer and I would prove justice. I had pictures from the bank with my husband withdrawing on my empty accounts. There was so much to do; it was a constant up and down, back and forth. My lawyer was doing his work and I continued to do mine, and I had all our papers in order. I was excited and anxious to know that soon the divorce would be over, but I was so nervous because I didn't know what to say, do, or think. This was new for me.

The hearing was scheduled which allowed me time to decrease my nervousness. It seemed as though everything was happening; my sister was coming, the car was acting up again, I had to report to Army drills, bills were piling up and my daughter was trying to decide what college she wanted to attend. I felt as though as if I was being pulled in all directions. I was extremely exhausted and although I tried very hard to deny it, my body was looking and falling apart. I knew once my sister arrived I would feel better, she was what I needed, a blood family member. My husband was becoming a thorn in my side. He tried to exercise visitation rights to his convenience. He would come to the house with his girlfriend way after the scheduled time and demand to have our son. This went on for a while, until I became firm. After the divorce, he has a difficult time getting Garland for the weekend or take him to church for that matter. Our son only sees him when he calls or beeps him mildly putting it, 800 times. It was awful trying to explain to my son, the behavior of his dad, but as always, I tried to sugar coat it so he would not think any different. School was out and the children had leisure time, except for my two sons; my youngest son was being held back because he had missed too many days while I was overseas and my older son, who enjoys spending his summer days in summer school, once again repeated his usual ritual. Graduation was beautiful, my daughter enjoyed her prom night and she was chauffeured around town to a nice restaurant with friends; I spent a good amount of money. Lakisha had decided to visit her cousin in North Carolina and probably needed the vacation more than I did, so I recommended her to go and to have a good time, physically and mentally. Her vacation turned out to be longer than I had anticipated, so we had decided to meet her when we arrived in North Carolina if she didn't decide to visit home sooner. Summer was dreadfully hot; I somehow managed to survive it. It wasn't easy. There were many times and many days when I felt I couldn't go on and many of nights when I felt I could sleep through them all, but my faith in Christ gave me the encouragement, that I could do all things if I believed who would be my source for strength. I don't want to sound like if I was a super woman, but I allowed my faith to take complete control even when my days were at its lowest, when I wanted to trade all, but I needed to be that super woman. Sometimes I needed to be super woman, because I knew too many people depended on me. My inner thoughts sometimes wondered why life was so unkind and why I was not able to see into the future so I wouldn't have to suffer. There probably were times when I could foresee the future, but my emotional attachment altered my mind to think otherwise or simply deny the situation. Maybe I did see, but I didn't want to be labeled a failure and end up lonely, so I settled, and became blind by some things. I didn't have a high self-esteem, I though I had, and mainly because I feared being alone, so I settled for what was and not what could have been. I was working twice as hard, two full times jobs during the week and working for the health agency on the weekends. I was becoming and feeling physically exhausted, but I knew I needed the finances to continue my lifestyle. The children remained supportive, taking care of each other and me. I was working non-stop. There were times when I didn't know if I was coming or going. My short naps were restless and physically I was becoming worn out, but I continued to play the role of a super woman.

Unfortunately, my youngest son didn't pass summer school and had to repeat the same grade again. I was disappointed, but I knew why, and I tried to reassure him it wasn't anything he had done. My husband was being very stubborn; he refused to give me child support, so I had to continue working several jobs, juggling between the three. There were times when I would come home and lie across my bed and sob for hours before I drifted off to the sleep. If anybody had cried a river I did. I was tired. My husband was trying very hard to confuse me and tear me down or whatever his motive was, but I continued to pray and seek guidance from my Lord. One of the reason, I guess, I didn't break is because I had many spiritual friends, not our church member friends who had forsaken me. They had deserted me too; they had fallen from my husband's propaganda, probably because he was a deacon in the church and had a great acting ability. The summer months had passed quickly and the children would begin school in several weeks.

My children were going to New York for Christmas to visit my parents; I was unable to go because I had to work, because we desperately needed the money. This was one of my saddest Christmases. Luckily, I had layaway on their gifts way in advance, so it made it much easier. One of the reasons why I was sad, because this would be the first Christmas I would be alone. There was no Christmas tree; I had not put up anything to symbolized Christmas, no decorations, because there was no children and no food prepared-only an empty house. I was working non-stop; there were days when I didn't even notice the rest of the house, only my bedroom and bathroom. I would check the rooms periodically, but it always made me sad. Once my children returned from visiting their grandparents, we celebrated Christmas, but it was not as our usual, there was no spirit at all, but it was heaven to have them back in my arms again.

Chapter 29

Falling Apart

One morning, I was driving myself home from work when I began to feel light headed. I felt as if my entire body had gone limp. I ignored this feeling and continued listening to the radio station and driving. I wasn't quite sure what to do or what was really going on, I thought if I pulled off to the emergency lane no one would stop and I would die, so I prayed and asked God to allow me the strength to drive home. While I was driving, I felt a ton of bricks pounded on my chest. I began to become frightened, so instead of stopping, I increased the volume of the radio and continued driving my way home. The heavy weight on my chest didn't move, nor did it subside, so I turned the radio volume as loud as it would go. I thought if I did this, the Gospel music would allow my mind to concentrate on something else. Luckily I was able to drive myself home. The next thing I knew I was relieved, for some reason, the pain had subsided, but I didn't feel good. When I entered the house, my son said, "Mom, you don't look good." I denied his truth as to how I was feeling or looking, but I continued plan B, to take them school shopping as planned. We drove out to Mandarin to my favorite store and shopped until we completed our plan. I was still feeling bad, but I didn't want them to know just how bad I was feeling. While in Burger King, my son insisted I visit the hospital, but me being the monarch as I was, I said, I'll be okay, I just needed rest. Rest is exactly what my body was crying for. Taking my son's advice, after debating with myself, and what if they keep me, if I go to the hospital, and in knowing that I hesitated to make that decision, but I knew I wasn't at my full capacity and I needed to seek medical attention.

Once inside the emergency department, everything else was history. I was wheeled to the back, hooked up to plenty apparatus machines and intravenous devices were started. There were several of nurses and technicians all doing their own specialty, but it was all too quickly; before I knew it they were finished. It was not long after calling my doctor, I was placed on a telemetry monitor floor, they continued to draw blood several times through my fragile skin and veins, and a stat EKG was done. Somehow I had strength to call my job and tell them what had happened. I was afraid for my children and nephews, they would be alone at night, but to my surprise, my oldest son pulled the family together and took care of everything as if he was a grown man. Although he was the oldest there, his sister was up north visiting family. I did manage to speak with her and she wanted to come home, but I insisted I would be fine and convinced her to stay and have a good time. Oh how she needed this time away. I must admit, while I was in the hospital, I slept well. They would give me a sedative each night, and boy I would drift right off into twilight zone. After I requested to the nurses that I would prefer not to be awakening for vital signs, but it made no difference, the lab technician took their place before dawn. One evening, my son surprised me and brought my little one to see me. He really made my day because I miss seeing my youngest son.

After several days of blood taking, test taking, and playing mom by phone, I was allowed to go home with strict instructions with a follow up visit. I didn't have a ride, so I called one of my friends to pick me up. To my surprise, my husband did not visit me. I knew he knew I was hospitalized because my friend is his close's cousin and they would have definitely told him. I then realized my marriage was over, it was really over. From then on, I could not turn back. Before going home, I dropped off my prescriptions to get them filled. There was no one home when I got home, so I initiated one of the instructions and went right to bed, but that didn't last for long before I would start putting things back together again. I must admit, the house was clean. I didn't over do it, when I became tired I rested. I was scared of my failing health and I didn't want to repeat what I had just been through. My children were happy to see me and so was I. My youngest son wanted to tell me everything that had happened when I was away and I pretended to listen, but my mind was focused elsewhere. I finally had my follow-up and I was cleared of any arrhythmias, and stress free. My doctor scolded me, and ordered me to give up one of the jobs if it wanted to see my next birthday and instructed me to get co-dependent, a book by John Bradshaw. After leaving his office, I immediately went to the mall and bought the book. I knew what was wrong with me all a long, I was doing the job of four people and my body wouldn't allow me to continue. Somehow, the body has a way of letting you know when it is time to stop, just like nature. It was a hard decision I had to make, I had grown to love my second full time job, and it meant a lot to me if I had to leave it. I was the head nurse on a psych unit, but I also loved my children and my health more, and knew that resigning would be beneficial to all of us in the long run. I did struggle for some time about making a decision and so I continued to work, but I knew I would eventually be headed back to the hospital, so I did the best thing for all, I resigned reluctantly. I thought about the limited amount of money my family would have, but my Father in heaven had assured me, He would provide and meet all of my needs. For some time, I felt guilty as if I had betrayed my job, but it was only because I was co-dependent and was not use to taking care of myself. I began to purchase several more books on co-dependent behavior and I was beginning to shape my life back in order, thanks to my doctor. My undying obligation to help others, I decided to purchase more of self help books, as my doctor suggested and had mentioned, if I wanted to survive my next birthday. I was going through changes, but I didn't want my obstacles to hinder my growth.

If I didn't believe in anything else, I believe I could get through this, despite the odds that were against me and the constant tears that flowed sometimes without much effort. I guess I could say my faith was being tested of some sort and the why was not answered. I allowed myself to stay focus in the supernatural realm. I attended church almost regularly, except for those days when I had to work. Sometimes I often wondered in joyful amazement, how I made it through. The war was behind me I thought and it had led to such devastation of trials and tribulations upon returning home; but I was able to hold on to my inner self, my well being, I was a survivor and Desert Storm didn't kill me and I wasn't going to allow this part of the journey to make me lifeless. My gas always seemed to be on empty, but somehow I managed to get to church, received rejuvenation and go to work. I guess there is a true meaning behind faith. If you believe in God, he would do the rest. I can still remember vividly, while I was listening to a spiritual station, I heard the voice of an anointed woman. Her voice drew me near her and I felt uplifted and close, as if I knew her, but I had never met this woman, not in the earthly sense and if I had met her in the spiritual sense, I didn't remember.

    She continued to speak and in closing invited the listeners, including myself to call in for prayer. At first I jumped up and dashed for the phone, but I felt silly, but then in moments, I dialed the number and requested to speak to her. Her voice was stern, deep, but compassionate. Her words were strong, but yet strengthening. As I poured out my heart, she invited me to her church. She said she needed to see me. I openly accepted her invitation, but I wasn't aware, my gas tank, once again was on empty. She lived a good distance, practically on the other side from where I lived, I thought there was no way I could reach her without being stranded half way there. But faith prevailed again and I stood my grounds and before I knew it, I was in front of a white storefront church in a small plaza in a predominantly black neighborhood. The church was not at all fancy, like the one I was use to, but the few people that were there was friendly as they extended their hellos. As I sat and waited for the pastor to come, I gaze my eyes around and noticed the church was in its beginning stage. The few people that were there were putting the finishing touches to beautify it. From the rear, there came towards me a tall dark skinned medium frame built woman, no make up just plain, but her walk was unlike what I had perceive it to be by her voice. She walked upright with grace, but with much femininity. She approached me with a hug and introduced herself and staff to me. As they quietly became invisible, we sat alone. I felt as though she was my second mother, I somehow became connected as if I knew her all along. She seemed genuine and trusting, I didn't have any problem opening up to her. Somehow God drew me to her and she became my earthly protector. As we closed, and said goodbye, she handed me a small brown paper bag. At first I refused to accept it, but she insisted this was a blessing and if I refused, I was refusing God. As I got into my car and drove away, I could still see her in my inside mirror, until she was no longer visible. When I opened the bag, I gasped for air after holding my breath. I couldn't believe it, enclosed was $40. To me it seemed like a million as I approached the intersection, there stood a gas station to my left side. I immediately stopped and filled up. I had desperately needed this money, and yes, it was a blessing from God. When I arrived home, I shared with my children my newfound mother and the blessing I had received. That phone call embarked a long life time relationship that still exists today. We can now look back and joke on those times, but back then, they weren't so funny. As for me, I became a regular participant in her church and today, I continue to assist her from time to time when she needs me. There is nothing too great I wouldn't put on hold to be at her calling when she requested me. I am forever indebted to her, but all glory goes to our Father who made it happen. I was once in the valley, but now I've been made whole.

Most people don't really understand the spiritual truth and I am not writing this book to convince you, just truthfully sharing my experience of what I went through and hope you would be enlightened and curious to find your own spirituality and your own personal connection with your Savior. My children and I attended church frequently, more so me than them. There were revivals that were going on and I didn't want to miss any. Most of the time, I would leave church and go directly to work. This was my place to get them solve with the spiritual saints, to keep my mind focus instead of drowning my sorrows into tears and the what if. It was a good thing for me, I was becoming stronger, not so much spiritual, but as a human being. But in everything you do, there is always evil trying to persuade you to do otherwise. I will never forget the particular night, when I had gone to work all teary eyed and frustrated. I had tried to keep my composure, but I am sure everyone could tell I was having a rough time. After going across the house to another unit to receive strength from a spiritual warrior, I somehow felt better. I had carried with me a spiritual book, that I enjoyed reading by Brother Hagan. He always seemed to uplift me when I was weak at the wayside. He always seemed to put me straight and I usually was okay afterwards. After leaving work, I can say I was in good spirit. I felt rejuvenated and spiritually fed. I told myself when I arrived home; I was going to spend some time worshipping and praying to my father, I couldn't wait to get home. When I arrived home, I found my nephew and son sleeping instead of being in school. I knew this was of evil doing to steal my joy, so I decided not to get angry, but to be firm and patient, he was the author of this confusion, instead I awoke both of them gently, and said, "You guys need to be in school." There was no fuss or any behavior that would have warranted speedily discipline.

As they dressed, I waited for them patiently in the living room. I normally didn't check the mail earlier because the postman usually ran later, but for some old reason, I was prompt to go the mailbox, as if I was being hypnotized to go. After a few odds, I decided to go anyway, when I did, I received a letter from my husband, I don't know exactly what I was thinking, but I guess I was thinking that it would be nice, and maybe in the back of my mind we would reconciled, but instead it was written in cruel English. I can't write the entire content, but it said something like; I'm divorcing you and I will only give you $50 for child support, not to mention the no alternative, just plain cruel, selfish, and straight to the point. I still have that letter as of today and everything else that followed. That letter touched my heart and I was once again tearful and my joy began to leave me. After dropping the boys off to school, I went to a girlfriend's house for comfort and prayer, you see the evil doer knew exactly what I had in store to do, he knew I was excited about going home, praying and worshipping my Father, so instead, he tried to still my joy by having me find that letter. He couldn't rob my joy with my son and nephew, so he tried another tactic that would hit directly to the heart and I felt hurt, but I didn't waver in my faith. Once arriving home, I called another girlfriend of mine, who insisted to continue my plans, since my blessing maybe within reach. After doing this, it wasn't before long that it was in the evening I needed to get some sleep, but before I did, I knew I needed to pray. I didn't pray long, because time was definitely against me and I knew I needed to get some rest before work and I did.

As I left the house for work, I walked down a few steps, when all of a sudden I felt a slight push in the center of my back and I fell. There was no one there and I didn't stumble on anything. I was actually pushed. It was as if someone gave me a gentle push in the middle of my back that is exactly how it felt. I didn't say a word, I just politely retrieved myself and held back my tears as I entered my driveway and got into my car. It probably sounds crazy, but I tried very hard to fight off the tears. My right knee began to throb, and I was in excruciating pain, but I didn't want to give in to the evil spirit. I continued to drive several more miles, entertaining myself while I listened to the radio, until I heard a voice say, go ahead, drive off the road, he doesn't love you. I continued my destination, but the voice continued to toy with me, trying to convince me, God didn't love you, and how God didn't care about me, but I knew this was the trick of the enemy. He had tried so hard to win me back, but my strength and faith was too strong in Christ. I suppose you are probably in awe, for those of you who don't understand the spiritual rim or the supernatural, but it is real as day and night. However, I must admit, it has not been easy to follow a righteous path. Sometimes, it seems as though, when you live a sinners life, life seems so much easier, you do not have too many burdens or problems to carry, but then again, how can we truly measure, it seems as though a probability of problems are less, but how can we be accurate. I continued to drive and battled with the enemy, until I reached my place of employment with tears of endearment streaming down my face. I was exhausted. I had just won, I arrived to work safely. Wiping the tears from my eyes before entering the building, I felt a sigh of relief, I was finally there, exhausted, probably humiliated, but unharm. I walked into the unit when a co-worker, who eyes bulged as she pointed toward my knee, as she asked the question, what happened to you, stopped me. I wasn't sure what she meant, because I had denied my injury I had sustained earlier that I didn't get the chance to look at my pants. When I looked down, I noticed my pants were ripped to threads at the knee and my knee receiving most of the injury was bleeding and dried blood stained my pants. I looked amaze, but I wanted to run to my friend who waited my presence, as she stood in the medication room. I couldn't believe that gentle push would have caused so much damage, all I could do at that moment was to embrace her as I cried like an infant wanting to be fed. I allowed her to nurse my injury as her spiritual words comforted me. We talked about my drive here and the toying I was having with the enemy. She understood she was an anointed saint. I would have never guessed I would repay the favor years later. Her spiritual growth and righteousness would cause the enemy to devour her good son, my friend, causing him to take his life. She has a special place in my heart. Her willingness to share God was always her character. She was gentle, firm, but fair, and for those who never knew her or didn't care to, missed a dynamite person. Although she would probably grieve forever, her humble spirit still shined. I sometimes wonder if I had the dynamics of her angel spirit, I don't think I would be able to stand. Unlike my first mother, she became my closest confidant and I will treasure the friendship forever, Thanks! After talking with her, I felt so much better. She always seemed to have the positive words to say. It was her way of saying, no matter how it looked, there was still brightness awaiting me. I have kept those words of wisdom in my heart and when things looked gloomy those words, I've always seemed to remember, and there is brightness ahead. After that ordeal, I came to realize that there is such greatness and the greater I believe, the obstacles would surely come, and my faith will always be tested.

 I prepared for my sister's arrival; she would be arriving Tuesday, which is only several days away. I had so much to do, clean the house, prepare meals, and get my clothes ready for work. Everything I set out to do went well, although there were moments when beads of perspiration rolled down my face and my body part were moving as fast as I was thinking, as if I was in a race contest. Nevertheless, all the things were done and the preparation for my sister's arrival was completed.

 My sister was finally on her way. I was excited and needed her desperately, if she only knew my despair, I believe her temperament would have been calmer. The day had finally come for my sister's arrival; my friend would offer to take me to the train station to meet her. As usual, the place was crowded, people were everywhere, but through the crowd, I was able to notice a thin frame, model looking beauty with a smile of pearly white teeth showing on her face, and yes that was my sister, looking great as always. We embraced each other tightly and lightly kissed upon the cheek, hoping not to smudge our lipstick. I introduced her to my friend, while we headed towards the baggage compartment to retrieve her belongings. While enroute home, we stopped at a fast food eatery to get her something to eat. It had finally happened my sister was here and a relief of yes had overcome me, we were a family again, a small one, but being together meant so much more than size. After returning home and getting her situated, I showered and prepared myself for work, and yes I was scheduled for work. I don't know why I didn't request the night off.

Work was its usual, nothing exciting, just the usually repeated clients, who hope for admission by acting out. My buddy and I talked all night expressing my excitement about my sister's arrival. He was happy that I was smiling again and showing some happiness. He always seemed to care about my well being. He truly was a gentle person. He was indeed a special person. His loyalty and wittiness always seems to shine. His intellectual and open mind attitude always seemed to have the right answers to solve most of my problems. Once home, my body desired much sleep, so I checked on everybody, showered, prayed, and went to sleep.

My sister stayed home for a while before she decided to go job hunting. It was very hard for her to enjoy herself as much as I would have liked her to because my working schedule was crazy with instability, regular weekends. Nevertheless, I tried to do as much for her when time allowed. Sometimes, it was very difficult because she had a dominating spirit and always felt guilty if I was tired and couldn't supply all of her needs when she wanted it. My daughter's return didn't last long, she decided to go back to North Carolina until I arrived there but it turned out to be longer. Unfortunately, my sister was pushy and stubborn as well as my daughter, so they always seemed to conflict. I was glad of my daughter's decision and wished her well. After all, she needed some peace in her life and if I at that time was not allowed any, I wanted her to have happier times. Luckily, I had some close friends who at no cost volunteered to take my sister around to her needed places. My sister was lucky, it took her no time to find employment and no sooner after, she was changing things in my house. She first decided the room wasn't to her liking, so she re-arranged the furniture, but then she put in a phone and had a private number, never once seeking my approval. Nevertheless, I didn't fuss, I knew her personality and it would only cause hard feelings. I guess somehow she sensed my disapproval and not before long she decided to move out. I wasn't aware of her plans; it was a kept secret. One day without much notification, she and the children were gone. I was truly hurt, I had waited so long to see her and now she was behaving selfish and unfair. I tried to be a sister, but no matter what I did, it always seemed it wasn't enough; at least that was the information my parents relayed. I didn't want my parents to worry, but at the same I wanted to let them know just how she was behaving, but my heart and spirit wouldn't allow it. Of the many things I have prayed for, one of the things I had prayed for was the spirit of assertiveness, but unfortunately that prayer has been answered and some people find it rude. We eventually drifted apart and began to take control over our own lives.

  I started to take charge and concentrate on my divorce, doing much footwork to decrease the legal costs. Mediation was scheduled and a court date had been set, and once again, I was going to have my say, according to my lawyer. During mediation, my husband insisted he wanted custody of our son. I firmly and quickly expressed if he continued to seek this concoction notion of custody, I would definitely eliminate him, and I was angry and frustrated and didn't mean a word of it. I knew this was a crazy tactic to get him to quit and I knew I wasn't able to pull it off, but I certainly sounded like I was, somehow it worked, shortly after he dropped the custody battle. He was becoming more of an obnoxious pain. He would do things to irritate me. If life had to be made miserable, he certainly had the personality to do it. He would show up at the house two and three hours later than his visitation time and demand to take over. What made those moments most awful for me, he would drive practically in the driveway with his mistress with a smirk on his and her face, while we exchanged our son. Our son would come back home with him and his shirt would smell of female perfume. I must admit, this disrespect would boil my blood, but somehow I remained calm and sane, all glory to God through it all. I continued to take it in stride. Although I was hurting inside, I wasn't going to let him see me in that state. I guess what hurts me most of all, I didn't understand why he wanted to hurt me, all I ever tried to do was make a home for our family, be a good wife and mother and support him in anything he wanted to do. I could accept and understand his love for another woman, but what I could not understand and allow myself to understand was, why was he always trying to mentally abuse me. Unfortunately, I have not been able to answer that question, but I had rationalized many of answers. He didn't regard my feelings; he was cold and insensitive. He would just do whatever he felt like doing, even if it meant coming to the house with his girlfriend on his scheduled visitation days. Although, it was difficult for me to understand, it was much harder for a five-year-old to comprehend. This went on endlessly until finally we made our debut in court. The justice system was all I had left to depend on but it wasn't the winning that would complete my happiness; it was justice for my children and myself. I wanted it to be over and I wanted what was due to us. My lawyer was convinced that I had nothing to worry about, he was certain I had enough documentation to get back what was wrongfully taken and rightfully belongs to us. It was not all easy, I had to prove my defense, build my case in order to save money, sometimes I felt, I was the lawyer because of the many things I had to do on my own. In truth, my lawyer was doing a good job, but many things I had to do, so my expenses would be at a minimum. When it was all over, I felt betrayed and stripped of my dignity and pride as a woman. Justice was not honorable it seemed. Immediately, I wanted to pursue law school to help others. I started to gather all the pawn shop receipts and the utility bills that were in arrays, outstanding telephone bills that were contributed by my husband, including the $1400. one he made after our separation. There were plenty of days I was exhausted from the heat and the much explaining I had to do. For example, I went into the pawnshop looking for any valuables that resembled mine, especially my VCR. It was there, but the owner could not give any information of which the responsible person was that brought it there, unless I had a stolen police report. Once again, I found myself walking into brick walls. With a lump on my head and an excruciating headache, I continued my lawyer's role until I was exhausted of all the pawnshops in my neighborhood.

 Finally relaxing at home, with my tired aching feet positioned on the coffee table, the last thing I needed was bothersome bill collectors calling me but to my surprise it was the Bank representative and her call was greatly appreciated after giving me the important news I needed to hear. As mentioned earlier, my husband was withdrawing money out of various bank early hours in the morning, but the sad thing about it, he was taking more than what was available in the account. With much enthusiasm in her voice, she said, I needed not to worry any more about repaying the bank. She said, "We finally found a picture of your husband with the view of a silver Grey Mercedes Benz in the background. She went on to say she wanted me to come to the bank to identify the picture and sign affidavits to clear myself. Although I was tired and really needed those few minutes of solitary, I obeyed. It turned out the picture was of him and a relationship that once was malice between the bank representative and myself, became good friends, giving one another encouraging words and hope.

It was far from over, but the pieces were beginning to come together, at least I thought and felt like I was winning. I met with her days later and recovered the additional evidence I needed for the case and closed that chapter by signing the affidavit of false accuser. I was excited and informed my lawyer on everything I was doing. It would take weeks before the footwork would be completed and we would finally have my day in court. From the suitcase of evidence, my lawyer and I had accumulated; there was no way the verdict would not be in my favor. We felt confident that justice would work out on my behalf and when I became a little uneasy; my proof of evidence would overwhelmed me. Unfortunately, after months of sleep walking and gathering important documents needed to represent my case, justice denied my children and I no consolation. Justice had slapped me in the face hard, and I was too numb to feel it. A deposition was held prior to my court date, and at that time, my husband explained why a portion of his money was not made aware of. I had loved and trusted this man with my life, but when my lawyer disclosed hundreds of dollars he had kept secret from me, from his paycheck, I then realized I really didn't know this human being as I thought I did, I felt betrayed. For years I had taken care of health insurance, but since my husband didn't have any coverage the employer rewarded him several hundreds of dollars in each paycheck. When I did asked him what the code meant on his paycheck he lied, and for years he had secretly betrayed the family. I was devastated; to say the least, my mouth remained opened. My lawyer had pulled the sheet off exposing this person for whom he really was. Name calling is irrelevant? Then my lawyer also revealed a female child that he had claimed as a dependant, and then an unborn child was mentioned on his part in hopes of paying less child support. While we were separated, he had not given us a penny, not to mention he left with all the cars, leaving one car with no keys. My lawyer was my spokesman, so my mouth was sealed as he represented my case. Although I wanted to shout as loud as I could to let the world know I had been had, I was forbidden to interject. The deposition didn't last long, but it seemed, as if it took hours, I was glad when it was over. I was confident, but I still had that gut feeling that he would find some other strategy to relieve himself of paying the full amount of child support. As the verdict read at the end, I was not able to get full child support for my son, my husband stated that he was only working part time, but my lawyer re-assured me that all would work out fine once the evidence was presented in court, burden of proof. It seemed like years before our final day in court.

So much was happening in my life. My sister was becoming increasingly impatient, wanting everything now, until the point we had to distance our sibling relationship. My daughter was gone again and my sons were doing their very best to be supportive of me. I was very sadden my daughter was not with me, but I kept in touch with her via phone. She really didn't know exactly what I was going through, but one thing she did know I missed her and she was not here and that was not good. She opted to come home if the situation got out of hand, but I insisted that she stay and enjoy herself to the best of her ability.

My sons were all too helpful. My oldest son had grown up sort of fast, and I guess that is why he is more business orient today and have no problem handling bills and negotiating. There were no vacations planned and a possibility of relocation to North Carolina seemed within minutes away. While preparations were in the works, I began to pack, hoping to rid some of the things I didn't desire and with a small possibility of findings missing items that were dear to me, if they were not taken in the sudden departure of my husband. I was doing so much packing, working at night and trying to be a super mom when time allowed me, through it all. Some days seemed better than others and some days I felt like a true basket case putting it mildly.

With everything happening, I had found a new friend; it was crazy and almost comical how we met. I was driving home from work one morning when I noticed a red car fly pass me. I didn't think of anything, other than this person was mentally disturbed, enjoyed speeding, or was on an emergency call, but little did I know he would become an acquaintance. After he passed, I noticed he began to slow down as if he was waiting for me to approach him. When I finally caught up with him, I noticed a white piece of clothing hanging in the rear window of his car. My second thought was not only he was a speed nut, he was also a doctor. He looked at me through his side window and then smiled, and I began to speed up a little, because the only thing I could think of from that is, the man was a psycho. My exit could not come fast enough before I pulled off and approached the traffic light; when I observed the same car along side of me. As my heart palpitated I could only think this man is crazy and he is following me and what was I going to do? I tried to remain calm, but my heart was pounding many beats of fear. I had to think swiftly. One thing I did know that I couldn't go home and allow this person to know where I lived. I continued to drive on as if nothing was going on to lessen my suspicions. There was no letting go he still was on my trail, smiling as if he had a plan. I approached a small grocery shop and decided to stop there; I thought if he was going to do something, he wouldn't do it in front of a lot of people. I went inside of the store and browsed as if I was going to buy something, but I was stalling for time and thinking what to do next. When I left the store, the person was standing in front of his car door. As I began to get into my car, he said, "Good morning" and apologized for following me. He went on to say he saw something nice and wanted to make an acquaintance. I didn't know what to say. At first I was not at all flattered; I still had butterflies in my stomach. He appeared very timid and reserved. He was small in statue and was slightly taller than I, possibly approximately 5' 6". His face appeared harmless, so I decided it would probably be okay to exchange phone numbers. I didn't think anything of it, but afterwards I wasn't sure if it was the right thing to do. When I arrived home and told my daughter about the crazy person I had met, she thought it was funny and great. She stated that I needed a social life. I did need an additional outlet, but I wasn't sure if that was the right route to take, so I told myself to pray about it. Being guided by the Holy Spirit, I was given the green light.

Our first outing was at my oldest son music recital at school. He was a pure gentleman; he opened the car door and escorted me to my seat. I was delighted because I wasn't use to this type of treatment, as we woman tends to forget once we become permanent mates, we are taken for granted and we are no longer looked at as feminine and gentle being as we once were before. We're special. And if this type of treatment could last a while, I was going to enjoy it; I was not going to be selfish. My son played the clarinet as if he had many years of experience, unshy and attentive to his notes. I was so proud of him. After the recital, we had a bite to eat and I was lead to my door with no attachments, but there was one upset I was married and love the Lord and I knew this could only be a friendship. Expressing my feelings days after with my friend, he agreed this would only be right. Our friendship was magical. I thought about the revival I had been in and the things that were prophesied to me, that I would meet my husband, he would be driving a red car and there would be a boy child. Although, the prophet vision was spoken in detail, a boy child was missing, but this vision would be revealed at a very much later date. I inquired about the boy child, not because I was in denial, but because maybe my friend did have a son and was not yet prepared to tell me, nevertheless, our relationship blossomed. We saw each other almost daily and the times we were apart, we talked on the phone. Our relationship was as if God sent such a special person to me. He was indeed a gentleman, it had been so long since I was treated like a woman, and I was taken by awe. Many days had passed and I was enjoying life and getting my life in order. I was beginning to feel like a human being. I was enjoying socializing, taking to a movie, eating in restaurants, walking through the shopping malls, and my life was different than what I was use to. We became good friends and my children liked him and that was definitely a plus. Although there were times when they felt they had to be protected, they allowed his friendship to continue. Our time became limited, since I was busy preparing my case for my final hearing.

Although my friendship was fine, there was still a part of me that wanted to be with my husband, but I knew our getting back together was not going to happen. There was still a part of me that didn't want to accept it. I was still moonlighting 2-3 jobs, because I was not receiving any money from my husband. Trying to manage everything was putting a toll on me. Recently discharged from the hospital, I was not going to go back, so I needed to keep that in mind.

The court date was scheduled and my lawyer informed me to dress casual and conservative and I did exactly that. Although I did as I was told, it didn't make any difference, it was a beautiful day as if spring had no boundaries. The sun shined bright and the wind breeze was cool, as it gently breezed my face. As I made my way into the courtroom as with everyone else, I passed through the security protectors. The protectors assured security, I was free of weapon of any kind and contraband that would do harm, except my document and voice. Once through the protector gadget, I took the stairs and found directions by following the posted arrow lines. Once inside the courtroom, we sat around the table bickering and using strategy to defend our case, the judge excused himself and conversed on the phone, expressing his concerns for the up coming Saturday golf game. After he directed his attention back to our case, we continued to proceed with exhibit A and B. Unfortunately, I learned a lot from this and one lesson learned is never write anybody a letter expressing their need to spend money. If wickedness does not surface in a divorce, then think again; it does. Exhibit A was brought in and used against me. I had written a letter in response to his letter of the concerns, and the depression he was going through. He expressed how he was working hard, feeling sad and the lack of not spending any money. Of course, that was a bunch of loose diarrhea. Yet, feeling sorry and understanding towards his concerns, I wrote him back encouraging him to treat himself to a suit and whatever he needed to make him feel happy. Before I concluded the letter, I also asked him to buy me some perfume, so when I come home I can use them and feel sensuous again. Since I was lacking the female extra necessities, I wanted to feel like a woman when I returned home; after all being in the desert is no place for a lady. I longed for the time when I could go home and soak in a bubble bath or just a bathtub full of all feminine fragrance. So you see, he took small exerts from the letter, responding to his complaints and used them against me as exhibit A and B. What he tried to do and did was to send the perception that I was out of control when it came to spending money and that I stayed in the shopping malls. To the contrary, they were all lies, but the judge had no sympathy or empathy on my behalf. He wasn't even partial. His behavior held true to a male chauvinist, and he proved that whole heartily. Heated argument ricocheted back and forth of the walls of the courtroom, as my lawyer argued my case. My oldest son was called to be a witness, after taking an oath he told of the constant absence of my husband and his obsessions to rent limousines, town cars, and help his friends was his most priority. My lawyer face turned from pale to peachy red when the judge excused himself again to chat on the phone about an upcoming golf game. When the judge ended his conversation, he stated his closing arguments, which frankly he would have kept for to himself, except for the dissolution of our marriage. He looked at my lawyer and me, and denied any monies other than part-time child support, he concluded by saying, since we were married, the money I was suing for was considered marital assets. I was only suing for $5000, just enough to get me on my feet until my finances were stabilized and to say the least the judge was compelled to express his concerns and said, "You are a nice young lady, a smart nurse, and you should have more equity than you do, my advice to you is to stay out of the malls." I was devastated, I could not believe how insensitive and callous the judge was. With all the proof of evidence that was presented, how could he be so blind and unfair, and to top off everything else, my husband who did not speak to me prior to our hearing did say as he was leaving, with a nice big smile on his face, "Oh have a nice day." Ironically, the divorce was final at 3 p.m., the same time my ex-husband and I had taken our wedding vows many years ago. My lawyer and I were speechless; our faces were in awe. It was nothing the lawyer could say to me to make me feel better. I was minutes from crying and if I recall, I did break down after I reached home. My sister embraced me with a hug, as tears of disappointment streamed down her face and she dried her weeping indiscreetly, encouraging me not to do the same until I reach home. My lawyer face was flushed and all he could say was "I'm sorry." I knew he was trying very hard to be sympathetic, but all I could think of was my ex-husband had gotten away once again from responsibility. My face was plastic in disbelief and my words were shortened, as I wanted more than ever to get out of sight. My sister and I immediately raced to the car, driving off speeding. My sister tried comforting me, by telling me how better off I was without him, but I couldn't understand why God had let me down. I tried to think of what I had done to cause me so much grief in my life, why was this happening to me, all I ever did was loved this man. I couldn't believe he wanted and had caused so much pain in my life. All I wanted right then was to get out of Florida. I needed to start anew. I wanted to forget about my past, I also wanted to erase the hurt. I cried and sob until I felt my tears had overflow enough. What I needed now was peace within, emotional healing, and closure of a relationship, it's over.

Chapter 30

"Relocation, I Can Do This"

Days had passed and I was beginning to build my confidence back. I was initiating my relocation debut to North Carolina. My friend was helpful, but I needed to do this alone, for me. I needed to find myself and bring peace within and most of all knowing I can do this. The task wasn't easy, constant phone calls, work, and preparation was seemingly tiresome, but I knew this is what I needed to get the job done. The good thing about the preparation, I had been packing for some time which that made it easier. My friend was so supportive. He was there to lean on, to cry on daily as I made provisions to depart. Although he said he would follow, deep within my soul, if he did not, it would not have much difference, because I knew I was doing this for me. I cared for him, but I needed to love me again. I had sacrificed too much of myself, and for some reason, I was no longer a complete person, I was mechanically existing. My loyalty to Christ was still there, but I felt as if he had abandoned me and my faith was shaky. As days went forth, I stayed with my sister until I was ready to leave. It wasn't easy, she was into her own world and I was in mine, but as always, we knew how to come together when we needed each other. I continued my preparation, until I had only a few days left before I was to leave. My job was kind; they threw me a farewell party and gave me nice gifts. I was sadden, not because I was leaving Jacksonville, but because I was leaving behind mutual friends, some that were supportive through my entire ordeal, through the end. As the minutes and hours passed by, I wanted to do something special for my friend, so I decided to make him a tape full of my favorite songs, e.g. Luther Vandros, Bette Midler, and so on. To have him near, I duplicated his tape, so I would have one too, so when I played the tape, I will feel closeness.

The day had come it was Saturday and I was going to leave, to my surprise, my friend decided to escort and pull his car by the U-haul. My sister and my nephews said their good-byes with tears of mixed emotions. Oh, how I wished I could have taken them with me, but they needed to be together as my family did. Immediately I scanned the rooms, looking around, making sure I didn't leave anything, but I had taken everything I had supposed to. As we drove down the boulevard, I could not help thinking back to the times I had shared there. There were so many good times, as well as sad ones. I could vividly look back on my first visit here, oh how I was so happy. The town was so beautiful and I had made Orange Park our home. I could visualize myself when I first arrived here, the schools, shopping malls, and local stores were all within reach, and the people seemed certain of a community that was developing into something big. I remembered looking for houses and fell in love with this newly built townhouses, which we purchased for rent to own. Then I reminisced about my daughter's first prom, and me rushing to get everything she needed so she could look perfect and she did. So many good memories that I was leaving behind, but I knew it was for the best. Then I thought back to the times when things were so bad for us, that I had to send the children to Seven Eleven stores to get little packages of sugar, so we could have Kool-Aid, but now we laugh at those times, but they weren't funny then. I thought about my oldest son first recital and how his body stood erect as he played the clarinet as if he had many years of practicing. I was leaving now, I thought, to something much more rewarding. As I wiped a tear that had forced itself to escape, I thought about my ex-husband and how he had become ruthless and cruel, and how he has forced me to change. Then I came to the interstate, which would lessen my memories as I focused on the sign that spelled North. I silently prayed for a safe trip, as I journeyed into uncertainty of the unknown, but one thing I knew for certain, I was free.

The road wasn't as crowded as I had anticipated, but no matter how crowded or not, the state troopers were out there, hoping to find the individuals who were heavy on their accelerator. I fixed my seat, played the music, and put on cruise control as I steered the wheel down the interstate. After a few hours, we signaled each other to stop, fuel, chat, and get something to snack on. We repeated this ritual every few hours, until I looked into my rear view mirror and discovered they were not in sight. Then I checked my speedometer and noticed I was over the speed limit and probably needed to give them time to catch up. I continued to drive, but at a much slower speed, until I spotted the U haul in my rear view mirror once again. Our last stop was in the state of North Carolina. We had approximately an hour to go if we took the back road; the back road would shorten our time, because it was pure country with no lights. We drove slowly as we paid careful attention not to come in contact with anything, since my visibility was limited. We drove pass houses that sat far from the road, as their reflectors of yellow or red reflected their presence. It seems as though we owned the road, since there weren't many cars traveling on the road. Once in a while a car might drive past, blowing the dust onto my car. The road indicated we were getting closer, but it seemed like 10,000 miles to go instead of ten miles. We were finally there, and although the surroundings were familiar, I always seemed to get lost, so I decided to call my cousin so she could meet us. It didn't take her long to get there, along with the others, even including my daughter, who insisted she wanted to be present. We greeted each other with hugs and lots of kisses and small talk. My daughter smile was proof she was glad I was there. Oh how I had missed those big hugs, they have always seemed to comfort me and how she made me feel needed. But most of all, I had missed our talks. We were so close, I could always talk to her about anything and everything and she always repaid the same. Once everybody greeted each other, we were headed off unload things. Since we had come in late, I decided it would be considerate if we stayed at the hotel. My cousin insisted that we stay with her as planned, but I decided that it would probably be best if we stayed at the hotel. We went to my cousin's house and greeted the other members of the family. Shortly after, we left and went to my other cousin's apartment where my two sons and I would be staying until I found an apartment. Once we arrived there, we were hit with the awakening, the elevators weren't working and we had to climb four flights of stairs. It was to our best advantage to wait until tomorrow; maybe then the elevators would be fixed.

After a good night sleep at one of the nicest hotel, we hurried for some quick breakfast. Once our stomachs were full, we went back to my cousin's place to put our belongings, but to our surprise, the elevator remained broken and we had to climb the stairs. After unloading the important things we needed, we found a storage space and unloaded the rest of the things there. It was a beautiful day; the weather was cool, breezy, but not windy. You could feel the cool breeze brush against your face. The weather here was so much cooler than Florida. It wasn't muggy or humid, as what I was use to. The day was ending and my friend needed to depart, since he needed to be to work the next day. It was hard for us to separate because we knew we would not see each other for a while. Although we had both agreed to see each other every weekend, that words said was only good for the soul and calmness for the heart. Every hour was a departing moment and after several hours, the time had come. It seemed so difficult to let go, but we knew we had to. As he got into his car, I felt I had lost a friend, who had been so near. He was there for me, for whatever his reasons, he was my supportive hand, and now like everything else that was happening in my world, he was leaving. Our eyes pierced each other, as we both knew what each other were thinking. One thing we both knew was, we didn't want to depart and that was obvious, since many hours had past. His hazel eyes gazed into mine and I could almost imagine embracing goodbye. Nevertheless, someone had to be strong and the emotional drama had to stop somewhere. Unfortunately, this goodbye love affair could have lasted, but I knew he had a long drive ahead and the last thing I wanted was something bad to happen. I politely and firmly told him this would be a last kiss goodbye and he had to go. It seemed to work at first, but then the talks reversed and now I didn't want him to leave. This trauma went on for almost an hour, until he said, "It's getting late Loretta, and I have to go now." We embraced long and tightly, not trying to break any bodily parts. We kissed once again and the next thing I knew, he was in his car. He started the engine and drove off, as I stood paralyzed in a daze as I watched the car ride down the road. As the car became distance, I was only able to see the red back lights of the car, as they became smaller and smaller, until they too disappeared. My friend had gone and now I was left to start what I had begun. I knew my new found roots wouldn't be easy, but then again, I knew I wouldn't be hard either, I had Christ on my side and he had never left me alone yet, well not for any length of time. I looked up to the sky, took a deep breath, exhale and said, "Yes I can do this."

Chapter 31

"Finding Peace"

A good night sleep is what I needed, I felt rested. I didn't have much planned that day. I had already had a phone interview for a job in Raleigh, NC. before I left Florida and I wasn't scheduled for orientation until the following week. I didn't hear from my friend and I was very much tempted to call, but I decided to wait until his time allowed. I did manage to organize my children clothing and put things in their perspective places. Once I finished, I decided to visit my aunt.

My aunt and I weren't close, but we became closer after our family reunion many years before. Actually, I was much closer to my cousin, who life ended while I was overseas. Her opting for single elective laser surgery to remove her gallbladder caused her eternity with Christ. Nevertheless, when I did visit, which was often, my family and I were always welcome. Although, I love North Carolina: I can confess, North Carolina has never been the same since her death. For some strange reason, it always seemed like something was missing, whether it was her smile, her gentle concern for others, or simply her conversations. Maybe it was her spontaneous adventurous personality that blossomed others when they were down or made you curious, just because she had that affect on people. For whatever the reasons, it didn't matter any more, she was no longer physically a part of our world, but her spirit always seemed to linger. I was truly amazed, how her only daughter was adjusting; she was handling her death very well. It was almost as if she was in total denial. At times her behavior seem, as though, her mother wasn't dead, because her daughter and family seemed to go on with their lives, as if nothing at all had happened. But with faith and endurance, God is not impossible;

he will take the pain away and shed new life on the wounded. But for me it was difficult because I now had lost a dear friend, who could no longer make me smile, laugh, or talk, all I had was memories, that I had to hold on to.

    There weren't a whole lot to do in Wilson, North Carolina, but it seemed as though everyone knew where the eatery places were and so we spent most of our time eating. My children were adjusting, but not as well as I had anticipated them to. They were missing Florida and their friends, but in time, I was sure that void would be fulfilled with some new friends. My friend had called me and we talked for hours. It always seemed as though you have so much to say when you are at a distance, but when you are together for some reasons, the words gets lost, but one thing we did confirm was his next visit and my golly, I couldn't wait. Although I had a job in Raleigh, N.C. I was forced to seek closer employment since my car decided to give up on me. My car needed major repairs, timing belt including the valves, and I needed to get major money. Everything seemed to be going splendidly well, despite my car problems. I was happy and at peace with my self. This serenity was long over due, but somehow I managed to enjoy my newfound beginning. My children began to find their places, making new friends, seeing the sights, and for the most part, not missing Florida. My new job was almost in walking distance from my house. The people there were so much friendlier than what I was use to. They welcomed me with whole heartily assistance and warmth. My children and I was beginning to find solitude, a grounding place, no fusing, and unneeded worry. My new job as supervisor was special, the staff made me feel special as if I was so some un-earthly special human being doing a job that almost anybody could have done, but I guess because my commitment to work many late hours and coming in to work many early hours showed dedication, they were not use to. I completed the care plans and MDS's, (Multidisciplinary Data System) that were logged for many months, for the state inspection, the job was grateful. Although, I was having the time of my life, I was not as fortunate to enjoy the many sights my children were seeing. But my nightmare would soon come to haunt me; my husband demanded his summer custody of our child. It seemed as though he would haunt my life forever, as long as our son was of illegal age to determine where he was finding peace, so I reluctantly prepared my son for his summer with his dad only because I knew of his false intentions and what would happen to me if I didn't agree. Luckily I had to put up with seeing him for a short while, but even that was too much to bear and old memories of pain began to surface, but with the help of my God, they quickly ceased into sweet memories. My son hugged and kissed us goodbye and a tear rolled down my face, because he didn't understand he was so innocent. I prayed that night that the Lord would pierce my son's heart and allow him to see the heartaches his father would cause. Although it was a selfish request, I knew he would hurt him, just like he had hurt my older children and me. Nothing unusual had changed; I was working hard, but not as hard as what was I was use to. My friend of a distance was keeping in touch and wanted my hand in marriage, and I was excited because he was special too, but I wasn't sure if that was the right thing to do. It just was too soon and I needed to make sure he was the right one from God.

Work was great, we had passed JCAHO inspection and everybody wasn't walking on eggshells anymore and I was recognized for a beautiful job well done. My director of nursing was well pleased too.

My car was ready and we decided to retrieve it, and get some soul food while we were out. Once we arrived there, the place looked empty as if they were closing, but there was a man inside and he decided to let us in. He smiled at us and took our orders. He was handsome, about 6' 2" or maybe taller, and looked like a real Carl Malone, but of slightly lighter skin tone. He introduced himself to me and asked if

I was from the area, for some reason, I had not yet developed a southern accent. My northern dialect always seemed to stand out. He ended his conversation with guys, come back to visit and we left all agreeing we would.

North Carolina was everything I had imagined it to be. It was greenery and wholesome, and the people there showed much hospitality, although the indifferences stood out. Everything was looking great, my children were having a good time, I was enjoying work and meeting pleasant, positive people and God was blessing. I knew God was still on my side, because things were happening that was not of me. I went to Fort Bragg (military base) for two weeks for my Army annual training, and acquired new friendships for life. They were super to work with and to be with. I was fortunate and very blessed; I met a Major, and she extended her warm welcome by inviting me to her house for the duration of annual training, along with another friend, who opted for the invitation. We were single, except one, full of energy and most of all, spiritually incline, which made our stay harmonious. We had such closeness that we prayed every day together. The Major was such a cook that she made gourmet dishes just about every night. We were inseparable, we prayed together, ate together, and stayed together, including going to church together. When quiet time allowed, we went our separate ways to complete our task. The strangest thing happened to me one morning while we were praying, my spiritual gift started to manifest itself (call it what you want, but I know it as the **HOLY SPIRIT**, it is real). I started to utter in tongues (unknown spiritual languages, written in the "Book of Acts") and began to prophesy to one of my friend about her husband. God began to show me a vision of her bedroom, which I described vividly to her, without ever being in her house or in her hometown in Roanoke, Virginia. I gave accurate description and color of her curtains, and bedroom including the eyelets on her bedspread. I described her husband who I had never seen, not even a picture of him.

I spoke to her about the changes God was doing on him right now as we speak; and as I write, I can still visualize him as he laid in the middle of the bed with his hands stretched outward on each side. I told her of their new truck they were going to receive, including the color. Two weeks later, her husband had made significant changes in their relationship, and they brought a new truck and the color was precisely the same as it was spoken to her that morning. It was amazing, she too was in awe, and so was I, only because, I knew in my heart it could not have been any body else, but the great I am. From that day forward, I became the little great I am, and for those who knew about it, and wanted to hear a word or two from God, came my way. However, God doesn't work in our time, He works on his time and where our needs are the greatest, and sometimes He came forth and sometimes he allowed me to be still. Life was beginning to look good for me, I had met wonderful friends who were spiritual and full of positive guidance, and I finally felt I was at peace; I was free of unwanted and unnecessary frustration that had engulfed my life for so many years. When AT (annual training) was over, I went back home only to find God was miraculously doing wonders in my life. He had given me a gift, a gift of prophesying. I know it might sound strange, especially strange to those who are not believers, but this story was intended for those who would allow themselves to open up their minds and see the spiritual realm as well as an inspirational awareness of my journey from war, trials and finally peace.

    I was at work one day, when one of my co-workers came to me and expressed some concerns about her life. God was awesome, he was really working miracles in my life, he allowed me to prophesy to co-workers on the job and to my surprise, everything that I had prophesied had came to pass and it didn't take years to see, only a matter of days, sometimes less than a week. Sometimes I would prophesy in the morning and by the afternoon, people would come back and tell me exactly what I had said, had come true. Although it was an amazing gift to have, I must admit, sometimes I was frightened because of God's awesome exact abilities. No matter how frightened I may have been, I was having a good time. Endlessly praying day and night, God was magnifying my gift, and pouring his spirit in me, and healing began to surface. One of my co-worker's moms was ill and needed medications, but she was unable to get them because she didn't have the money. After praying for her and her mother, God also allowed me to prophesy to her. She too had desired many things patiently, and had wanted a China cabinet and needed a car, but with most of us, finances didn't allow. But after praying with her, God had informed me to tell her the desires she had wanted was about to come forth. By the end of the week, her husband brought her a China cabinet for their wedding anniversary and drove up to their house in a brand new truck; now that is incredibly awesome, God is real. Although it seemed impossible a few days ago, it certainly came to pass in just a few days and as far as her mother, she became well. As with everything life was so grand and my tenor in North Carolina was about to come to an end. My daughter was a pre-med student at one of the prestigious colleges, but I was unable to afford the tuition there, because she was not a resident, so a decision was made to return to Florida. I wasn't happy about the decision, but as a mom and many prayers, I didn't want to stand in her way or her career. But before I could gather our things and leave, I had to accumulate money. I talked to my friend in Florida and asked him to look for an apartment and to send me an apartment guide. Our relationship was great; we had become distance, probably due to a phone call I received at work from a woman informing me, he was engaged to marry her. Sometimes men can be so callous; majority of them can't be trusted, because they always feel the grass is greener, always chasing a thrill. I was disappointed, but like I told her, "I'm engaged to marry him also; I guess he's the marrying kind." When I talked to him, he denied it and made up some pitiful story that he let someone used his car, and that is how she found my phone number. Although I allowed him to think everything was fine, my heart had paralyzed and my feelings I had for him. Luckily, I found solitude and comfort in God, who would never forsake me. I must admit, I wasn't settling for wooden nickels, so the hurt did not linger and I went on with my daily routine, putting forth the positive attributes that needed front line attention. It's really kind of sad that we put our trust in man, but we must put our trust in God because he never fails us. It is also good to pray and ask God to send you a mate, because sometimes what we desire is not always what we need and God always have a better plan for us. My newfound soulful man was there also and I took advantage of his laughter and conversations to past the time away. Although we were having the time of our lives, walking through the park and acting silly, I knew it would only last for a moment.

I sat down with my children and we decided on what day we would be leaving. We had moved out from my cousin's apartment and moved in with my son's girlfriend's mom. Everything was going great, we were going to church and I was still working, but all I wanted to do was to leave, mainly because her oldest daughter was out of control and had no respect for her curfew or for that reason anybody else. Unfortunately, the days went by slow and two weeks seemed almost like a decade. We were planning my son's girlfriend's barbecue and since she was so nice, I brought her some school clothing. My son had special balloons made for her with a teddybear inside a huge plastic, it was pretty. We left all of our belongings in the car in the shopping mall parking lot to find my daughter some shoes, a passer-by decided my car needed to be cleaned out, and robbed us of all our belongings, including the battery cables, my daughter's purse, and camera. I was devastated, and received no help from security. It was a definitely loss and I duplicated all that was stolen. That situation had dampened my spirit and violated my privacy, but I was not going to allow the incident to spoil my day nor my spirit. Plans went on as usual and the barbecue was great.

Our departure was coming near and we exchanged phone numbers, addresses, and said our good-byes once again to all as many as we could. One thing we did have was memories, as I think back, some were sad, and some full of joy. I could remember when we would have to drive to Greensboro, North Carolina, when we needed money, because there was no ATM machine that would honor my card. Greensboro, North Carolina, was about an hour drive through the back countryside of North Carolina. Sometimes my daughter and I would listen to the sounds of her favorite singer, Keith Sweat, "Make It Last Forever", because she would die if she didn't, but then there was joy, laughter, and most of all each other. Then there were the sad times, when my oldest son came running home from the park because some boys wanted to jump him, but nevertheless, the time spent there was all good and well worth it.

Chapter 32

"Returning To Florida"

We packed our belongings and headed for the road. There wasn't much talk because we all felt some sense of loss, but we were returning to the south, we all knew once again. My ex-husband was informed of my return and was instructed to return our little one as planned. We were two hours away, when the car decided to slow down on its own, I thought it was because I was using the cruise control, but I wasn't using it at all. I stared and tried to pull over into the median. With my hazardous lights on my hood up, I thought that would be a great indicator we were stranded, but to my surprise, people were scared to be generous, and no one came to our aid for a while. My son tried everything he knew, as if you couldn't tell him, he wasn't a mechanic. I was scared straight and getting wet because it was raining. I didn't know what to do, and I didn't want anything to happen to my children. Once again, I prayed silently to my Father in heaven, asking God for safety and assistance and as always, he always provided our needs. The sun had faded and darkness was beginning to prey upon us and no one stopped to help us. After about thirty minutes, a blue car drove passed, then turned into the median and backed up and headed in our direction. We sat quietly as if we couldn't believe our eyes, someone was stopping, and God had answered my prayer. It was hard to see who the person was, because the glare from the motorist headlights beamed steadily as they traveled in opposite direction. He was definitely of African decent. Not being bias, or for that matter prejudice, he was very dark skinned, tall, and scary looking. He wore a ragged tee shirt and blue jeans that reminded me of the navy sailors with wide pant legs way above their ankle. His hair was curly and looked very oily, he had Jeri curl and there was no style, just a do. He spoke as if he didn't have the respect of grammar school, but he was our help, and we were glad of that. He asked me what was wrong and I explained what had happened; he too wasn't sure what the problem was. One thing he was sure of, he said he was headed for Kentucky but said, he knew a friend in town that could help us and he would take us to Dunn, North Carolina where he lived. I wasn't sure if I was making the right choice, since my mother always warned me, never go with strangers. However, I knew it was one of him and four of us, including God, so I opted for the assistance and he tied a cord to my front bumper and to his back trunk, and told me to steer, as he slowly drove down the highway. Although it seemed forever, a few exits before he drove off into a truck stop. The truck stop was huge and isolated, with only a few trucks that sat in its spaces. I was beginning to get scared, and asked him me if he could pull me into the hotel down the road. He didn't seem hesitant and that was a good sign, but for some reason, he thought we would be safe there, and for some reason, I thought we would be safer at the hotel. He obligated my offer and we drove to the hotel. I thanked him for kindness and offered him some money, but he wouldn't take it. He said he would call his friend so he could help me. I wished him a safe trip to Kentucky since his car looked and sounded like he needed a major overhaul himself. But nevertheless, we were safe, stranded, but safe. I called my mother and told her what was going on. I couldn't think of many people who would help us, and besides it was too much to ask of them. I called my ex-husband, but not to my surprise, he wasn't helpful, so the only thing I could do was to wait for the stranger to come and pray. My children were hungry and anxious, so my daughter decided to call her friend for assistance, but the bad thing was we didn't know it would cost $60 and the manager gladly informed me to pay now or find another hotel. At that point, what could I do, I had no other choice, I was furious, but I knew she was trying to be helpful. The question always surfaced why is it when you are going through, it seems as though everything is coming at you all at once? Well, I'm sure I can answer that, only because that's how the devil wants us to think. He wants us to think that there is no way out, and there is no light at the end of the tunnel. He wants to weaken our spirit, and once our spirit becomes weakened, then we can no longer look beyond the blessing that is about to come, and continue to focus our faith in the Lord. I think that's the way life is, molding us into better people, so when crisis occurs we are equipped to handle them. For one thing, we became stronger, and able to stand life unfairness with boldness, but when we are going through, it seems so impossible at the time, and that is why faithfulness is so important. I don't know why so many things were happening to me, but I can say this, I can walk through the fiery darts with much ease now, minister to others, and I have been able to overcome almost anything. I guess we human beings of spiritual faith, are tested to see how deep is our faith, since good deeds without faith is obsolete. It is so much easier to say I love the Lord, but are we able to stand the tests: and endure many days of agony and hurt, are we able to go through the fire like Daniel, are we able to be manipulated, are we able to stand in honor of our Father, and prove our love for him, and wait on the Lord to see us through. One thing I am absolute of, God is always at your side, even though he allows us to go through life unfairness. Yet He gives us strength to go through those times and overcome anything.

As I rested on the bed to regain my thoughts, there was a knock at the door, and to my surprise, the stranger had arrived. I can't say I was scared anymore, but I was definitely apprehensive and watchful of his every move. He introduced himself and so did I and I led him to the car. He popped the hood up and manipulated wires, plugs, gadgets, and then turned to me and said, I think it's the valves. He said he would order the parts I needed in the morning and go from there. Of course the answer was always okay, since I didn't have a choice.

My son found a Burger King across the road and went to get us something to eat. I'm not fond of Burger King, but I didn't have other options. I was in Dunn, North Carolina, and I didn't have a clue of this small town. We watched some TV, took our showers and headed to the bed.

Morning couldn't have come sooner, as I waited for he mechanic to make his visit. He definitely had to be Christlike, because his light shined with kindness and compassion. Although I doubted at times I knew in my heart, God never sends anybody to help you not of his spirit. He treated us to breakfast, what else than Burger King and then we headed to the auto part store. He said he would have the car ready tonight, but with all plans and the way life had been treating me, that wasn't happening. The bad news was, the auto parts store was closed and he wouldn't be able to get the part until tomorrow, well that was great. I had to remain in Dunn, NC for another day. The problem with that was my funds were getting low and I didn't know how much the parts would cost. Nevertheless, I paid for the next day in advance. Lakisha called her friend to meet us at the mechanic work place, but this time it was billed to another number and not at the hotel. We were to travel with him somewhere in the country, where the car would be fixed. The next day, we went with the mechanic to his friend's house to fix the car. It was definitely a country road, surrounded with many trees and plenty of woods. I was scared once we approached the house. All I could think was, we were going to be kidnapped, chopped up into pieces, and buried somewhere in the woods, but I guess I was watching too much scary television and seeing too many scary movies. As we got out of the car, a few dogs ran up to make their present. As I looked up, a white male came out of a trailer looking straggly and unkept. All I could think of was how I got myself into this. As he came near us, he held a big huge knife in his hand; my heart literally skipped a beat. He greeted himself and tried to comfort us about the dogs, they were big shepherds. He left us while we were waiting with Mr. Smith, as he proceeded to work on the car. I had immediately told Lakisha to call her friend again.

There was no way I was going to allow us to stay here without another male present, she did and he was on his way. The atmosphere was creepy, and as I looked to the right, I noticed a run down shed. I was frightened, but I didn't want my children to see that I was. It would only add to their apprehension, but one thing I did know that if anything was going to happen I was going out with a good fight. The white man came out again, this time holding a knife and a big huge watermelon. He laid it on a ragged table that stood in the yard and in need of many repairs and cut the watermelon in half. He offered us some, but at that moment, we weren't eating or drinking anything. The white man chatted with the mechanic shortly and went inside his trailer after inviting us in. We stood around looking, just like we felt lost. The mechanic worked on the car, pulling parts apart. After a while, he said, you are not going to believe this, I though the car was a four cylinder, but instead it is a six cylinder, that's why he had to reorder the correct part. With much concern and lack of knowledge about cars, I went on as if I knew exactly what he was talking about. After a while he encouraged me to go inside the trailer to relax and insisted I was in good hands and I would be fine. He stressed the wait might be a while and he wanted me to be comfortable. At first I was reluctant only because of memories of scary movies, such as, "Jason" and I didn't want to be in a vulnerable state and jeopardize my children, but I was getting tired of standing around, so I decided to take the chance. Inside the house was plain; nothing excited, but old CB equipment that was treasure by the owner. He talked on it as if it was the latest model, but it was his pride and joy, and he talked as if it was. Nevertheless, that's what brought him comfort and relaxation, so I understood. I can say he wasn't a person of decorative imagination. He was simple and the old used sofa and a torn tavern throwaway chair was evidence of that. Although his trailer was simple, it was comfortable and clean. You could tell he lived alone. There were no major appliances in the kitchen and no pictures of memoirs on the wall. The only thing visible was a used toaster and well-preserved pots, except for a pan of stale grease that remained in the pan. His hospitality continued, wanting me to taste his smoked sausage that he had preserved from his shed. I did try a very small piece and must admit it was good, but chose not to try another. Trying to make myself comfortable, I sat down in the chair and tried to watch the TV, but my anxiety level was still at large and my eyes remained wide open.

After an hour or two, my daughter's friend came to our rescue, just like he said he would. Although his visit was shortly, he definitely made sure my daughter and son had something to eat. After an hour of being still, I decided to check on the mechanic and the status of his accomplishments. The engine sat on the ground as if it had no house and the mechanic faithfully worked as minutes were turn into hours. His face showed confidence and a joy to his work and he continued as if I wasn't there, but when time permitted, he did acknowledge me while he worked. While he worked it allowed me time to be grateful and thankful that I had met someone who was safe. Time became my friend and as minutes ticked away, I was honored to know the Lord had truly had His hands on my life. I went back into the house, but this time I wasn't afraid. The darkness didn't allow you to see much distance in front of you, unless a light was beaming. I chatted with the old man and enjoyed his stories of yesterdays and this time I was attentive. We laughed and chatted and time was of essence as if it slipped into darkness to the wee hours of the morning. My children returned and my car was completed. Although it was 4 a.m.

in the morning it was a glorious blessing because we were once again on our way home. We said our good-byes, hugged, and exchanged numbers hoping we would see each other again. My mechanic refused any money and said once I get home, I can send it then when I get straightened out.

As we journeyed onto the road, our vision lost sight of them and I knew he was my angel God had sent. As I played sweet music and thought of how long I had to go, I looked at the rear and my children were sound asleep. My next stop would be South of the Border, a chance to refuel, get coffee, visit the restroom and stretch, in all that is what we did. I was illiterate when it came to cars, it sounded good, drove well and all I wanted it to do was perform well so I can get home. Welcome to Georgia, I knew I was close, but yet so far away. I drove while my children slept. Welcome to Florida, I was almost there, but I would not allow myself to feel joy until I was at my sister's house. Although, if anything happened now, it was okay, because I knew I could call someone for help. When I arrived in Orange Park I was relieved. I had done it, we had made it despite the odds and I looked to the sky to tell God, "Thank you."

My sister was waiting and she was over joy, but I knew the happiness would not last forever. She was different, unlike me, born in the same world, but we both had different views, just about everything. I knew I had to get a place quick. It wasn't before long, I found a place and job, and things were looking swell. I was beginning to find myself, but shortly after, I was laid off, but with perseverance and determination, I needed stability, and not before long I found a new job. The apartment wasn't what I had been use to or for that matter, what I expected, but it was ours, and that was the most important thing. I spent many days cleaning, preparing, and fixing up. I wanted it to be just right for my children. My youngest son was coming home soon and I was glad we were going to be a family again. We moved in shortly and the children were excited, they once had their own rooms again and we were away from the frustrations that made its way into our lives. However, it was not way near what we was use to before my divorce, but it was comfortable, it was ours. However, what I wanted most was stability and felt I was finally allowing myself to excel. My children were excited once again. They also were gaining stability and having their own room made them very happy. I think their privacy was desperately needed and they wanted that more than anything else. My friend assisted with our move, helping me clean and prepared for our new beginning. I knew I really didn't want to be here, but I knew I had to except my arrival in a city that had caused me so much grief. While I knew I had to build a tolerance again, I also knew I had to convince myself I was doing it for my daughter and she meant more to me than my pride. Many days went forth and I began to settle in. Life seemed as though it was going well, until I went to work that evening. I was called to the Don's (Director of Nursing) office as soon as I had punched in only to be told, things aren't working out and she no longer needed my assistance as the assistant director of nursing. I couldn't believe what I was hearing, my face looked like I was in shock, dumb founded, so I asked her what she had meant by that, and she said, "Things aren't working out and I don't think we would get alone." These words of despair penetrated my soul and were beginning to be a part of my life and I was becoming too familiar with them, but once again, I reminded myself, this was the south and some people were quite different. However, maybe it wasn't the south as much as I wanted to place blame, maybe it was me, I was different and everyone around me knew this, I thought, or maybe it was a greater power I was fighting against, the devil himself. One thing I was certain of, God wasn't going to put no more than what I could bear, and so be it. I can't remember how quickly I left as I did, but I do remember me fighting back the tears, so satisfaction could not be rejoiced by the enemy. The streets were empty and it seemed as though I was the only one. I began to pray and questioned God's wrath as I had thought why was my children and I suffering so much? Why was I burdened by all life's difficulties of unkindness, God always reminded me of Job (a disciple in the bible that went through long suffering but survive). So many thoughts were clustering my head and one of them was how was I going to tell my children, I had failed them again. You see, I couldn't see any brightness that night, I didn't have trust and my faith was withering as I allowed myself to be angry, and I was angry. I didn't want to think of anything or anybody for that matter, I just wanted the pain to go away. I just wanted to be normal again, if there is such a word. Once in my bed, I covered myself from head to toe, trying to escape the pressures that had engulfed and consumed me.

Chapter 33

"Reality Shock"

Morning was always beautiful, as the sun slowly emerged making a break through, as it beamed against my window, as the glare bounced off the blinds, as if to say, "Good morning." I knew I had to do something, that the bills would come in and they needed to be paid, so job hunting became a part of my life. Although I was working odd jobs at the health agency to keep afloat, and the war was beginning to be behind me, I was beginning to become my old self again. Although my friend was kind, he was not helping me financially, so I had to do it by myself. I was working so much; there were times when I didn't have time for my children, because tiredness would get the best of me. Then the big job came, I landed a job 80 miles from my home, it was full time, paid good, and had good benefits, so I accepted it, I had to survive. The only problem was transportation, but my friend was willing to get me there and back with no difficulties. Eventually, I looked for a roommate and shared a room with a stranger. Our union was good and we had a few things in common, except that she loved to hang out and have a good time and had many men visitors, which led me to put the dressing drawer in front of the door before I went to sleep. Although the job was beautiful, I missed my children deeply seeing them over the weekend wasn't good and they really didn't have much supervision, except for my neighbor, who looked out for them when I wasn't there. Not long after I resigned my position so I could be closer to home, but I needed to do what I had to do. At times I felt quilty about it. I asked my friend to get out of my life, after finding several love passion marks on his neck, which needed no explanation from him and not to mention he was engaged to someone else for seven years, including me. At one point in our lives, we continued to remain friends, but I have not seen him in several years.

I didn't have any steady partners, I was dating and seeing people, but no one seemed to elevate me. I continued working for the health agencies, working whenever they needed me, until I landed a full time job. Everything seemed to going well, but once again, my hours declined and I found myself out of work.

Unlucky with finding a job and hitting bottom, I filed for unemployment. I thought I was cursed because my life seemed as though it had taken a turn for the worse, my bills were mounting, my car was repossessed, after I called them to come and get the piece of junk that stayed in the repair department more than on the road. I was becoming frustrated and it had begun to show. It seems as though anything I tried was crumbled before me and there was no way out. I called my old co-worker, a good friend who was like a brother to me and he tried to cheer me up, but his words of wisdom were useless, because I wanted change now and change wasn't coming. I remembered hanging the phone up and crying uncontrollably, finding myself in a corner of my room, sitting on the floor, crying out for mercy, I was at my wit ends and I had hit bottom and I needed the comforter and I needed it quick, and as always he came. The feeling of being held had emphasized all the feelings a man could give to a woman. The comforter warmth was of great essence and it did exactly that, comfort. It was something of amazing about the Holy Spirit, but you first must be a believer to know and understand. I knew from that moment I wasn't alone and my Father never had left me and it was good to know and feel. As I sat there being illuminated from his love, I prayed to God to send me a help mate, a companion, a friend. I told myself, I was no longer going to look for Mr. Right; I was going to be patient and wait on the Lord. I gathered myself together and looked at myself in the mirror, as I saw myself looking at me; I began to minister to myself. I was alive. I was able to see, feel, touch, and I was still bless. I had survived the sands of Saudi Arabia; I had been spared the attack of the Scud missiles. My children were also healthy and I had so much to live for, and so much to receive, and I thought how selfish I could have been. Even though I was having periods of diarrhea, insomnia, upper respiratory infection, and an unknown rash that would surface on my right upper arm, that was beginning to happen to me after the war, I was still blessed. I pulled myself together and thank God for His peace and His mercy, and for ministering to me. Many days had passed and I was still unemployed, but with much respect, my bills were getting paid. Prosperity was beginning to happen; I landed myself a good job. I was employed full time and my bills were being met. Life started to look up for me and my hope was restored. Greater things were happening, I had finally found peace within the tornado hold that once had me bound, and Christ has continue to be my source of strength. I have newfound energy now, and a greater need to exist. I have traveled many miles before but now I was traveling on the path of righteousness, my willingness to encourage others that life does not have to be a lost to a stronghold, but can be a beginning to a greater supreme being that supercedes all others if you believe in Him . . . He is our protector and comforter in all crises, although He may allow the fiery darts to toy with us, He will never allow it to succumb us. We must have faith, and never doubt the great I am, for He is always by our side. As we travel through life we will be offended by many unwanted obstacles, but we must stand firm to our faith, and the process will flow smoothly. Life can not and will not always be easy, but if we seek the knowledge of our Lord, and hold on to His promise, then all things are possible, and our reward will be in **HEAVEN**. This month was my annual training with the army and the good news; I would be training here in Florida for two weeks. At the end of my two weeks, my sister invited me to a boxing match, doing nothing exciting; I thought that would be great, so I accepted without much hesitation.

Chapter 34

Finding My Soulmate

I was excited about going out; it had been such a long time since I had been, so I pampered myself on what to wear. I fumbled through the closet looking for the right outfit, until I narrowed it down to a flare skirt and top. To my satisfaction, I wasn't please, so I looked for something more appealing, until finally, a pants and top was my final choice. The event wasn't far from the house, so I raced between getting dress and trying to do something to my hair. My sister was to meet me at the house, so I had plenty of time, she was always late. I added my final touches, earrings, bracelets, and of course perfume and I was complete while I waited for her arrival. The club itself was big and the smoke film room clouded the top of the ring where light was most visible, it was crowded mostly men and a handful of couples. We had front row seats as we watched the boxers bounce at each other, as the sweat covered their faces, they both looked intense, but nevertheless, only one could win. The doctor stood beside the ring, waiting for his cue, as if he knew he would be called upon. The crowd roared and yelled for their favorite, and I yelled too, not knowing who was the champion, just screaming for the one who threw the most punches. Having a good time, I decided to go to the bar to buy a can coke and as I approached the bar, I stumbled on a medium size black male. Unable to see his face well because the lighting was dim, but the smell of his cologne radiated with essence. Somehow, I knew in my heart, he was my soul mate. Most people would argue the fact that love at first sight doesn't happen and can't be possible, but I felt sincerity within my heart, but I didn't know how to pursue it. You see, I am from the old school and girls just don't ask guys out, at least that's the way I was raised, but I know time has changed since my raising, but I still don't think I would have the nerve to do it. His smell directly asked me to pursue it and then he said hello. His hello was awesome. His voice had this innocence about it, but yet boyish and sexy without him putting forth any effort. We chatted to each other and for some reason, I was so intertwine in him that for many days, he was known to me, and called Jeff, later finding out his name was Jessie. I tried very hard not to act as if I was desperate, but deep in our hearts, we were both were shy, so our conversation was limited, but we were able to find out what each other did for a living. He was self-employed and I hinted to him to do a job, but he wasn't buying it, unless I paid, but it was all in conversation. I never had any intentions; I just wanted to know him. We said our good-byes and he vanished off into darkness as if he never existed and I went back to my seat in a total daze. I didn't know whether I would see him again, but I knew somehow and some way I was going to find him again. I told my sister of my new soul mate and she had no positive answers I wanted to hear, but she did say her friend knew him and my prayer might be answered. Her friend was so into the match that my desperation was not of importance at that time to him. Several matches went on, but all I could do is think of my new soul mate, where was he and what was he doing, and who was he with, luckily I'm glad I didn't know at that time because my heart might not had accepted it. But to no avail, he was there somewhere in the dark, but I was unable to spot him out. When the fights were over, I left, not knowing how I would ever again get to know him. I thought of him constantly, but it was obsolete, I would probably never see him again.

Once again, my sister invited me out and to my surprise; my soul mate announced himself, buying all at the table all drinks. I knew I couldn't allow him to get away this time, so I had to think of something to do and fast, but what could I do, I thought? I didn't want him to think less of me, so what could be better when his cue, "I'll get in touch with my sister's friend," I quickly jumped in and said, "if you can't get in touch with him, you can certainly get in touch with me and I will get in touch with him for you." Although it was quick, I couldn't believe I had just given a man my phone number, but what the heck, it has paid off to be heaven and I love every minute of it then and now. A few weeks had passed and I didn't hear from him, but then it all came together.

One night while I was writing in my book, I received this phone call, and it was he. I was flabbergasted; I had to tell him to hold on while I held my chest to keep my heart inside. I was amazed; he had finally called me. When I returned to the phone, my thought was to ask him what took him so long, but instead, I changed the words a little, so it wouldn't look obvious. We chatted a long time, while I melted inside. We talked about family, work, food, people, ourselves, and as a matter of fact, he invited me out that evening, but I had an interview the next day and was unable to take him up on the offer. I almost had to force myself to sleep, we were making a connection and I saw the green light to proceed, of course I prayed about it and didn't hear anything otherwise, so I was going forward. I wanted so much to call him today, but I didn't want to be pushy, so I waited for his call, and when he did, he invited me out to the movies and I accepted. I was happy, he had fulfilled the void that had so long been missing in my life, a true companion, but I wasn't going to move fast, just enjoy one day at a time and left God be in the midst of it. He picked me up as plan, and we watched the movie, and then he later suggested on something to eat, but I decline, I was on my best behavior, but simply because I wasn't hungry, I was too excited and just being with him was all I needed to be fed. He was quiet, somewhat shy, and a gentleman. His shyness almost scared you, because he too was probably on his best behavior. His hands were soft and he spoke with such softness, that his eyes almost lured you into his world he was genuine. His words were positive and full of motivation. He became my confidant and he expressed how I should outline my book and I took his advice and it has been easier to write it. He was what I needed and if this was a dream, I didn't want to wake up, never. He wanted me to see his house, so he invited me there. At first I was skeptical, because I didn't want anything to spoil a good beginning, so I said to him, you know I'm a brown belt in karate, and don't let me have to experiment on you, he chuckled with a smile, and I laughed, but I still was little on edge, but I went anyway. His house was large, and it included a pool as he showed me around. The furniture was simple, typical of a bachelor, but clean. He was excited too, but he tried to be cordial, so he played some music, why he insisted I see videos, which consisted of him jumping out of a plane, bungy jumping, and dancing with his best friend in New York. He was awesome and full of adventure. I believed this was his way of telling me who he was without words. Before I could ask any questions, he was fast asleep.

Many days thereafter were lovely, not only had I found my soul mate, but also I had found a friend. We spent many moments together and every time he thought of me, I would get a surprise present. He was special. Halloween was approaching and he had this costume party to go to, so he wanted to be Barney, so I found a Barney costume for him, and Barney he was. Although I was not able to go with him, I did get a chance to see him after the party, but it was okay, because I have this trust that no one could stand between us. His behavior and mannerism did not change and we were inseparable to a point my daughter was curious and asked, "What was he doing to me." It has been a few months and I felt it still wasn't time to bring him inside my house, so we continued to court, as if that was not a problem and never once did he ask why. He probably thought it was something else, but the real reason, most of my furniture was in storage in North Carolina, and I felt uncomfortable not having my house complete. Later on as our relationship blossomed, he made arrangements and took me to get my furniture. He is everything a person would want in a mate, and later has become a part of my family. My children have accepted him, as if they knew him for years and believe me that is an honor.

He has been a positive force in my life, encouraging me to finish my book and scolding me when I procrastinated. He has been a father to my children and has gone through the suffering and pain, teenage problems has caused. I am honor to have his love and I am honor to have met him. God has blessed this union despite the odds, and has given me a new outlook on life that nothing is impossible if you believe in God.

Chapter 35

"At Last"

It is easier to throw in the towel and take the easy way out, but if one believes in God and has faith, nothing is too hard to overcome. I have come a long way through the sands of Saudi, scud missiles, betrayal of love, lonely nights, financially broken and lost friends, but I have learned to master all despair through God's love. He has shielded me against the fiery darts and has comforted me when I need so desperately to be love. There is no easy worldly life, but to be born again, you must encounter trials and tribulations. There are times when you are burden with such trials, that you tend to remove the full armor of salvation, which shields you from disaster. Then one might say; why must I go through it if God loves me so much, then I say to you my friend, it is faith that keeps you strong and God's love that guides you towards eternity.

My life is much calmer now and I have run a good race in what this life holds for me, I don't know for sure, but one thing I am certain of is everlasting life. May God speed be with you all, and remember when you're going down that dark tunnel say to yourself over and over again . . . "Yes I Can".

Epilougue

War can be and is vicious in how it destroys lives. However, we must be reminded that individuals can destroy lives too, and we must not excuse them for their malice and vicious behavior, but find peace within our spiritual realm to forgive them. This story is not intended to destroy or put the military down in any form or fashion or to exploit the players as they were. No war can ever be organized, no matter how equipped in technology we think we are, we are still human beings and many lives are still lost, whether it be physically or mentally, because there is a greater power other than ourselves. I wrote this book to encourage others that meet life at its hardest, and to encourage those who struggle through obstacles and have found themselves frustrated and burden by life's uncertainties. I hope this book brings positive awareness and energy in a spiritual realm, and to assure all readers of this book that struggles are not lasting, and you can survive life's hardest obstacles if you believe. Prosperity comes to those who are enlightened to me. My journey to Saudi Arabia has been a learning process; it has taught me to grow as a human being and to appreciate the simplest things in life. I view life at a different angle, although coming home was hurtful, but through it all and through Christ's strength I have found my inner peace and a sense of belonging that in order to survive, you must know who you are and what your purpose is in life. I believe in order to be successful; one must also have failed at something else. If you can leave this earth with just one accomplishment, then obstacles are okay, your living then would not have been in vain. Since then I have learned to love myself and appreciate the smaller things in life, that sometimes we take for granted, and I have also learned to appreciate the simplest things in life that some things are okay and if its okay with me, then its okay. But last there are supreme powers that are merciful and forgiving, who watches over us when we are not taking care of ourselves, and most of all they don't ask for much, and they are, God and his son Jesus Christ, who loves us unconditionally, even when others and we don't love ourselves.

So whatever you might be going through, don't give up, because there is hope, but most important you can receive salvation, it's your choice. So if you desire to seek salvation then here is your opportunity:

In Roman 10, verse 9 through 14, God talks to you about Salvation. "If thou shall confess with thy mouth, the Lord Jesus, and shall believe in thy heart that god raised Him from the dead, thou shall be saved. For with the heart man believeth unto righteousness and with the mouth is made unto salvation. For the scriptures saith, whosoever believeth on Him shall not be ashamed. For whosoever call upon the name of the Lord shall be saved. How then shall they call on Him in whom they had not believed? And how shall they hear without a Preacher." In Roman 10:13, the Bible says, For whosoever shall call upon the name of the Lord shall be saved.

Rejoice always, pray without ceasing. In everything give thanks; for this is God's will for you in Jesus Christ. 1 Thessalonians 5:16-18.

I am at peace now. So when your life is in a place that forces you to detour, just remember, "Yes I Can".

Abbreviation List

ALERT: READINESS FOR ACTION DEFENSE, OR PROTECT A WARNING SIGNAL OF A REAL OR THREATENED DANGER.

ACTIVATE: TO PUT INTO EXISTENCE BY OFFICIAL ORDER TO PREPARE FOR ACTIVE SERVICE

AK-47: A SOVIET ASSAULT RIFLE

AO: AREA OF OPERATIONS

APFT: ARMY PHYSICAL FITNESS TEST

AT: ANNUAL TRAINING

AWOL: AWAY WITHOUT LEAVE

BB'S: SMALL FOREIGN CIGARETTES... GIVING THE APPEARANCE OF MARIJUANNA JOINTS

BDU'S: BATTLE DRESS UNIFORM

CHAIN OF COMMAND: THE SUCCESSION OF COS SUPERIOR TO A SUBORDINATE THROUGH WHICH COMMAND EXERCISED

CNN: CONTINENTAL NETWORK NEWS

CONUS: CONTINENTAL UNITED STATES

CONVOY: A GROUP OF VEHICLES ORGANIZED FOR THE PURPOSE OF CONTROL AND ORDERLY MOVEMENT WITH OR WITHOUT ESCORT PROTECTION

CSH: COMBAT SUPPORT HOSPITAL (UNIT)

DEPMEDS: DEPLOYABLE MEDICAL SERVICE (FIELD HOSPITAL)

EKG: ELECTRICAL ACTIVITY GRAPH OF THE HEART

FORMATION: AN ORDERED ARRANGEMENT OF UNITS PROCCEEDING TOGETHER UNDER A COMMANDER

FORWARD AREA: AN AREA IN PROXIMITY TO COMBAT

HUMVEE: HIGH MOBILITY MUTIPURPOSE WHEELED VEHICLE (THE NEW JEEP)

ICU: INTENSIVE CARE UNIT

ICW: IMMEDIATE CARE WARD

JCAHO: JOINT COMMISION ON ACCREDIDATION OF HEALTHCARE ORGANIZATION

KP: KITCHEN POLICE OR MESS HALL ORDERLY

MASH: MOBILE ARMY SURGICAL HOSPITAL

MIA: MISSING IN ACTION

M 16: US MILI ASSAULT

MOBILIZATION: THE TOTAL OF ALL RESOURCES AVAILABLE, OR WHICH CAN BE MADE AVAILABLE TO MEET FORSEEABLE WARTIME NEEDS.

MOPP: MISSION-ORIENTED PROTECTIVE POSTERIOR

MOS: MILITARY OCCUPATIONAL SPECIALITY ONE'S JOB TITLE.

MP: MILITARY POLICE

MRE: MEAL READY TO EAT

NCO: NON-COMMISSIONED OFFICER (E-5-E-9)

OBS: OFFICER BASIC SCHOOL, A MINIMUM REQUIREMENT FOR ALL NEW OFFICERS ENTERING THE NURSE'S CORPS

OIC: OFFICER IN CHARGE

POW: PRISIONER OF WAR

PX: POST EXCHANGE OR AAFES

QUARTERS: GRANTED TIME OFF FROM MILITARY DUTIES AS PER MD

TA-50: ARMY EQUIPMENT

Myself and daughter-n-law Yolanda after her graduation ceremony at Ft. Gordon, Ga.

My son Garland (on the left), my oldest son Joseph (during boot camp at Ft. Jackson, SC), myself and nephew DJ (on the right).

Family portrait.

My mother Lizzie, and my sisters Kyshindia and Lakivea.

My grandson Joseph II (also known as LJ), myself, and my father Lonza.

A Special Thank You

The Swinney-Scott family would like to say "thanks" to the following for their support in seeing that this book was written.

Dora Battle
Steven Cromity
Kirk Daniels
Ernestine Dial
Jessie Ferrell
Emma Gillard
Dale Lucas
Emma Lee
Lizzie Swinney
Carol Turner

I would like to express my gratitude to two great authors. **E. Lynn Harris**, thank you for your support, and encouraging words through experiencing of writing with expression. To **Mary Monroe** for your unwavering words that said, "I can," I thank you for your support. Your gracefulness has encouraged me to express my thoughts and uncanning imagination through the stroke of a pen to success, thank you.

I now reside in the State of Georgia with my younger sister. I remain active as a Registered Nurse and U.S. Army Reservist. My two older children have married and relocated, with one son preparing to leave for Iraq this July. I am a proud grandmother. My love for writing continues and I continue to be an active believer in Christ.

TO ORDER ON LINE, LOG ONTO:
WWW.XLIBRIS.COM,
OR VISIT MY WEB PAGE AT
WWW.GULFNURSE.COM